Dear Mama

Stories of an Extra Lucky Life

Taryn Lagonigro
Jessica Quarello

A Four Clovers Publishing

Four Clovers Publishing Registered Offices: Caldwell, NJ 07006

Taryn Lagonigro & Jessica Quarello
Dear Mama: Stories of an Extra Lucky Life / Taryn Lagonigro & Jessica
Quarello

ISBN: 979-8-9853136-1-1 (Print)

979-8-9853136-2-8 (Kindle)

Published in the United States of America. Book cover design by
Morgan Silva.

While the authors made every effort to provide accurate information at
the time of publication, neither the publisher nor the author assumes
any responsibility for errors, or for changes that may occur after
publication.

This book is a creative nonfiction. The information and events in this
book are the memories of the authors and the writers within. The events
have been expressed and written as remembered by the author. Certain
names and identifying details have been omitted to protect the privacy
of individuals.

*This book is dedicated to the members, parents,
and caregivers in the disability community.
And to Cindi and Terry, two moms who showed us
what advocacy and unconditional love
was from the start.*

Dear Mama,

Thank you for picking up this book. Whether you are here because you are new to a disability diagnosis for your child or are already part of, or connected to, the disability community, we appreciate you.

The women who wrote these letters are some of the most inspiring mamas we know - in part because they opened their hearts here in the hopes of helping someone else through their words. They are women who may have lacked what we are hoping you find here - knowing someone else "gets it." We hope that in one of these stories you find *YOU* - someone who has felt and thought things you're feeling now. Often in a journey like this we feel very alone, but we are here to tell you that this is a book full of women who are very much here for you. They were where you are. They love their babies to the depths of their soul *and* still can feel very hard feelings. Most importantly - they are okay, and you will be too.

The only thing we asked of any of our writers is to be as honest as possible. You'll get to hear the good and the hard, the very raw feelings but also a whole lot of hope.

This book was a true labor of love. The hundreds

of hours of planning, coordinating and editing was done with the mission of putting something out there that would both support moms as well as start much needed conversations about what needs to change – whether that be diagnosis delivery, support that families are lacking or the mental health issues many of us face as we walk this road. Change comes from vulnerability, and we know you will find that in the hundreds of pages to follow.

Thank you for being here.
You've got this.

Jess & Taryn

Contents

Dear Mama

Stories of an Extra Lucky Life

Letters 1-7

LETTER 1

Extra Lucky Jess

Dear Mama,

I'm so glad you're here. I'm going to be bold and assume that if this book is in your hands, you're in need of solace and support. You may be scared, anxious, in shock, fearful, disappointed in your new and confusing circumstances AND absolutely in love with your child. That's how I felt anyways when I received my daughter Adeline's Down syndrome diagnosis moments after she was born.

I coined the "And Concept" which has been really helpful to me as I navigate this journey as an extra lucky mom. Before I go into exactly what that means, I think it would make the most sense to introduce myself and share our journey. I want to let you know that this story is going to be raw. I don't want to hold back because vulnerability ultimately leads to connection, and I want you to know that I have felt ALL. THE. THINGS. *AND* still love my little girl with all my heart. So, here is our story:

Adeline was going to be our last baby. She was going to be the missing puzzle piece that took our family of three to a family of four. If I'm being transparent, I hated being pregnant the first time, and I hated it even more the second time around. Despite friends, mothers and experts alike ensuring me that every pregnancy was different and that my second pregnancy could be even better than the first, I was SO excited to NEVER be pregnant again, because it most certainly wasn't better...it was actually worse.

I was diagnosed with cervical spinal stenosis in the summer of 2019. That said, when I got pregnant in the fall of 2019, my neck was in a decent place. I wasn't dealing with the horrible chronic pain that had plagued me for months and the medication regimen I was put on by my team of doctors was actually working! I was really excited when I saw those two pink lines on the pregnancy stick. I knew it was a girl immediately in my gut but the way I felt was so different I assumed it was a boy. When I became pregnant, I had to stop my medication regimen completely, cold turkey. That's when it all turned kind of black for me. The medication took a few weeks to leave my system and once it did, I swear I could feel the bulging disc hitting my spinal cord at every look, turn of my head, and especially every time I picked up my precious 2-year-old daughter. To use an adjective to explain the pain, I guess I would say it was tremendous. By week 9 of my pregnancy, I was absolutely suffering. I was in so much pain I could barely function. I remember holding a knife in one hand while cutting up vegetables for dinner and looking at my left forearm. I wanted to slice it open. I wanted to be in control of the pain in my body for once. I remember dropping that knife and crying out to my husband. I sobbed as he held me, completely helpless. Luckily, my doctor referred me to a prenatal medicinal doctor who prescribed a lower dose of my previous medications. My baby was going to be closely monitored for growth through monthly ultrasounds. I would be able to get through the pregnancy and my baby was going to be OK. This was January of 2020, and by March 2020 the pandemic hit. To say that my pregnancy experience was stressful would be an understatement.

Despite the pain I experienced throughout my pregnancy, I felt a weird sense of calm and strength throughout. My baby girl had passed all her testing (my gut instinct that my baby was a girl was right!)

and she was healthy. She was growing on track despite my medications and as my due date neared, we became more and more excited to meet her.

During my 8th month of pregnancy, I had gained 50 lbs and carpal tunnel had reared its ugly head again as it had previously in my first pregnancy. I started dropping things and noticed severe numbness in my right hand. This was concerning to not only my OB but to my neurosurgical team as well. They were worried that the weight of my body and baby on my spinal stenosis could create irreversible nerve damage. We all agreed that my baby girl would need to come 3 weeks early via c-section.

Baby girl's due date arrived, and the excitement was palpable. I was so ready not only to meet this little lady, but to finally celebrate the end of what had felt like the longest most painful pregnancy of all time!! It was July 21st of 2020 and my family had arrived to care for our oldest daughter, Charlee, who was about to become a big sister. My husband and I had been covid tested a few days before and were able to be together in triage. We drove into Manhattan from Hoboken to Mount Sinai West in NYC swapping daydreams about what this little girl may look like and what personality she may possess. Would she be spicy and sweet like our

Charlee girl? Or would she be the total opposite? We checked in, I got dressed into my hospital gown and basically skipped into the Operating Room. My first delivery experience was a vaginal birth so the OR was a little intimidating. Everything was white, sterile and smelled extra gross like that clean hospital smell. I took a big breath and allowed myself to be a little nervous. I assured my inner voice that the weirdness and uncomfortability of that moment would pass soon enough once my baby girl was on my chest.

Once I was on the table, I met my wonderful anesthesiology team. They were so kind and calmed me down almost immediately. Matt came in shortly after in scrubs and was able to sit right next to my head which calmed me down and lowered my blood pressure. There was so much joy in that room. It was almost tangible. We were so excited! My anesthesiologist and my OB made sure that I was in fact numb from the waist down and then the c-section began. I really could not feel much at all! It was kind of crazy. I felt some weird numbness and tugging but honestly that was about it and I was prepared. Less than five minutes after the c-section began, my OB asked if we were ready to meet our daughter! She raised her up over the curtain and this adorable floppy baby with long arms and legs peeked out. Everyone screamed "Congratulations!" as Adeline Blake Manna Quarello cried out. Adeline was brought over to the incubator to get her weight and vitals checked while Matt rubbed and kissed my head. My OB kept mentioning from behind the curtain that my low back pain I had experienced during pregnancy was due to the position of Addie's head directly against my pelvis. She also mentioned that her head had a flatness due to this as well. She kept repeating this over and over, and it started to become a bit alarming. What was also alarming was how long the vitals check was taking and the fact that the energy was literally zapped from the OR. You know how you can enter a room and hear a pin drop? Yea, that's what it was like. I was still on the table being sewn up when Matt was asked to come over to the incubator. A few seconds passed and the next thing I heard was "I think I am going to pass out. I need to sit down." Then my husband was swiftly escorted out of the OR, and I was alone on the table. I was totally clueless as to what had happened and assumed that Matt had seen my belly open on the table and got sick. I even made a joke out loud to my anesthesiologist by saying "See! This is why women have the babies! We can handle anything!" I still cringe remembering that those words came out of my mouth.

Typically, if you pass out in the OR you are not allowed back in, but somehow my husband was able to come-to and ran back in less than five minutes later. He looked like he had seen a ghost. When he sat down beside me, I asked him if he was OK. He grasped my hand, looked me straight in the eye and said, "They think there is something wrong with our baby." To which I said, "There is nothing wrong with our baby Matt. Her face has a bit of flatness because of where she was positioned against my pelvis. Our baby is a perfectly fine babe!" He looked at me with a face that used to haunt me. You see, he knew what was "wrong" with our baby. The pediatrician that had been called in to take a look at Adeline had told him what was "wrong" with her, but he didn't have the heart to tell me. I'll never be able to thank him enough for sparing me my hope. It wasn't the right time to learn of a birth diagnosis and he knew it. He protected my heart at all costs, which I guess to me is the definition of true love, our love.

Adeline's oxygen was not where they wanted it to be so they had to take her to the NICU. I asked if we could at least try and take a quick family photo before they took her away. Ridiculous I know, but they obliged and we took our photo. I was never even able to touch her before they took her.

Once inside the recovery room, Matt told me that the doctors thought Adeline had Down syndrome. She was showing a number of physical markers and had hypotonia, or low muscle tone. What I learned later, but didn't know then, was that the pediatrician on call that day had essentially accosted Matt with this diagnosis in such an aggressive and insensitive way that he blacked out in the OR. The moment Matt came over to meet his daughter, the doctor had pulled Adeline up by her neck folds and said "See. Your daughter has Down syndrome. She has extra skin behind her head and neck, she is floppy…" as she flipped her over. I could go on, but you get the picture.

I went into a kind of shock. I was in denial. I was empty. I had literally just been cut open and I had no baby in my arms to show for it. I was emotionless for a little bit. I just couldn't believe it and I wasn't going to believe it. I looked down at my feet and saw my husband's body laying across my legs, heaving up and down. He was sobbing. I had never seen this strong and capable man I loved so much, so broken. That's when the screaming started. I couldn't breathe but yet I was screaming. "Where is my baby!!!!!? Where is my baby???!!!" I screamed over and over and over.

I don't know how we got to our recovery room. I

honestly have no recollection of that transport whatsoever. That's the funny thing about trauma. You have no control over what your brain wants to remember or how your body will manifest what it does. It's been over two years and so far I don't remember but maybe one day I will, who knows?

I didn't get to meet my daughter until she was 18 hours old. Because of covid, women with c-section deliveries couldn't go to the NICU until they could walk there themselves, so you better believe I walked my ass there the moment I could. It took me 25 minutes to go down one long hallway, but I did it.

When I approached her incubator she was sleeping. She was so beautiful despite being covered with wires and the oxygen that was taped under her tiny nose. I loved her immediately and I was sure that she did not, in fact, have Down syndrome. I would spend the next three days walking down that long hallway to the NICU to see my baby, continuing to convince myself that she did not have Down syndrome. I would inspect her every limb for these stupid "markers" the doctors claimed she had. That is until I met an angel. Well, her name was Angel, and she was Adeline's nighttime NICU nurse. I asked her one night if she thought Adeline had Down syndrome, and this is what she said to me: "Jessica, it does not matter if she does or if she doesn't, because she is a human being who needs to be loved by her mother. Just hold and love your baby. Feed your baby. Give your baby the gift of being her mother." Her words rocked me to my core. What have I been doing all these days?! Inspecting every inch of my child?! Worrying about a diagnosis??

I stopped inspecting Adeline and decided at that moment that no matter what the karyotype test said, my love for her would not be rocked.

The next day we received the results, and it was understood that Adeline did, in fact, have Down syndrome. I had already fallen in love with my daughter so I was able to accept her diagnosis. I was no longer in denial. It was hard but I got through it and each day after as I got to know my precious daughter more and more, I started to see Adeline first before I saw her diagnosis. Isn't that how we should see each other? The person first, and the skin color second. The person first and the disability last? It should be that way, but typically that's not how it goes. I look forward to helping change that.

Adeline is now two years old. It's been the most earth-shattering time of self-discovery I could ever have anticipated. The things that I used to put importance into are simply less important. Adeline works so hard to do the things I take for granted. She didn't walk until she turned 2 and yet watching her work so hard to get there made the wait BEYOND worth it. Her joy and perseverance is an inspiration to all of the lives she touches. Is she my last baby? I can proudly say "Yes!" There was a time I felt like I would need to have another child to fill the void of a "typical" sibling for Charlee. What I can tell you is that the relationship between my two girls is arguably more beautiful than a typical sibling relationship. I know Adeline will make Charlee a stronger and more dynamic human being, just like she has made her own mother. Adeline is not the child that we had originally imagined and envisioned for our family, AND that is OK.

What I can say now, two years later, is that Adeline is so much more than her diagnosis. She is beautiful, courageous, strong, resilient, silly, spicy and sweet. She has forced me to change my entire life's perspective. She brings a beauty to our family that neither Matt nor I could have ever dreamed. She is a blessing. And she also happens to have Down syndrome.

The ignorance surrounding life with a child with a disability is astounding. I thought my life was over after receiving a birth diagnosis of Down syndrome. What

I have realized is that I am able to live a beautiful and full life with Adeline as my daughter. I can navigate this life of mothering a child with a disability my way. I can be Jess AND Adeline's mom at the same time. I can love Adeline while celebrating each and every milestone that she reaches on HER timeline AND worry about the future. I can do hard things AND struggle. We all can. This is the "AND concept."

The AND in this life is what I want you to understand is OK. We can love our babies and also have hard days and there is nothing wrong with that. It doesn't make us bad parents. It makes us human. Congratulations to you wherever you are on your journey. Wherever you are on that journey, I know you are extra lucky.

Jess Quarello

Meet Jess

Jess is a mother of two girls and a social media influencer, content creator and writer in the motherhood space. As the co-founder of the advocacy platform Extra Lucky Moms her mission is to spread the joy of disability motherhood which she does through the ELM platform and blog and her social media (@extraluckyjess on Tik Tok, @jessquarello on Instagram and her website jessquarello.com) She currently resides in Hoboken, NJ with her daughters Charlee and Adeline, and husband Matt. She hopes to inspire others facing a disability diagnosis to not fear the future but to embrace a new and beautiful perspective.

Extra Lucky Brianna

Dear Mama,

I know you're upset. I was too.
I know you're worried. I was too.
I know you're overwhelmed. I was too.

I remember all the feelings so vividly, even now, 3 years later.

I remember feeling so guilty about having those feelings, too, but in time I learned to get over that. I went through the normal emotions, the same ones all my Down syndrome mom friends told me they went through, too. I got through it with the help of my husband, my family and my friends. Although it wasn't easy, it helped me to become the strong mama that I am today - a mama I am so proud of.

We were lucky to get pregnant so quickly. In fact, we went on our honeymoon 7 months after our wedding and I had no idea I was already pregnant. I started getting the typical symptoms of pregnancy and went back and forth for a few days if it was just feeling a bit off from all the traveling or if I was actually pregnant. On July 25, 2019, the night before my 31st birthday, I took a positive pregnancy test in our hotel room in Sydney, Australia. We were laughing hysterically and crying tears of joy. A moment we will never forget!

It's crazy to think at that moment everything about our baby was already set – her gorgeous blue eyes, her funny personality, her beautiful smile, her tiny stature and of course, her 47 chromosomes.

We spent the remainder of our honeymoon completely ecstatic. We talked about names, we talked about how we were going to tell our family and friends when we got home, and we shopped for little souvenirs at a market. I swear my husband didn't stop smiling for the rest of the trip. He was so protective of me, constantly asking, "are you hungry? Do you need anything? Are you allowed to drink coffee?" This was all new for us and we were so, so happy.

A couple weeks after we returned home I went to my first doctor appointment. I was 8 weeks and we heard her heartbeat for the first time - it was perfect! We tricked our parents into coming over to see our "honeymoon pictures" the next day, when we really only had one picture to show them: the ultrasound picture of their soon to be grandchild. The screams could be heard throughout all of northern New Jersey.

At 14 weeks I received my first "abnormal" test result that showed our baby had a 1/13 chance of having Down syndrome. The genetic counselor called and left me a voicemail saying "Your results show a high risk for Downs, but don't jump off a bridge." When I called back she kept stressing that there's a "90% chance it won't happen!" In my heart I knew it was happening and I really wanted to be sure, so I went ahead and had an amnio, which confirmed the diagnosis.

I sat on the table and everything went black as we were told all of the "horrible" things that go along with a Down syndrome diagnosis. In one long, run on sentence we heard, "children with Down syndrome have a high risk of leukemia, heart defects, early dementia, low muscle tone, they have a shorter life expectancy, think of how this will affect your family and your future children, couples get divorced over this." I don't even remember the rest. I just sobbed and my husband sat beside me and held my hand. We were so scared, not to mention, a week away from our first wedding anniversary and already hearing the word "divorce".

We were then led into a room down the hall where we were told we had "options". I was upset, hysterically crying and apparently very naive. I finally mustered up the words to ask, "like what?"

"We can set you up with an appointment in the city." I said, "for what?" She bluntly stated, "An abortion." I cried even more. She said, "I will send you in to see a doctor, he will put you to sleep, open up your cervix, and remove the fetus." I angrily said, "AND THEN WHAT?"

This is the baby my husband and I talked about & dreamed about. This is the baby who surprised us on our honeymoon and made our trip even more unforgettable. And now someone is suggesting I get an abortion?

Those first few days and weeks were the hardest. It was right before Thanksgiving, and right before our first wedding anniversary on December 1, 2019.

My husband was so strong the whole time. His confidence made me believe that I could do this, that WE could do this. We knew it wouldn't always be easy, but we would do it TOGETHER and it would be so worth it.

We celebrated our one year anniversary the next week and went out to a nice dinner. I had barely been to work since we got the diagnosis because I was constantly crying, and honestly, barely functioning. The next couple of weeks were hard, but there started to be good days again, too. I knew there would be good days, but I really believe I had to go through a grieving process. I'm not embarrassed to admit that; I was worried about my baby.

We initially said we didn't want to find out the gender, but at this point I wanted to know so I could get the nursery ready, shop, and feel as ready as possible even though so much seemed out of my control.

I had gone to the doctor's office to pick up the envelope with the gender in it in the middle of December and put it under our tree. On Christmas morning we opened the envelope with our parents there to celebrate. It read: "A girl! Congratulations!"

Our greatest gift.

We officially decided on her name the next day: Sydney Rose. Sydney for the place where we first fell in love with her, and Rose to pass down my middle name. The tears were finally stopping. This was our baby girl, our Sydney Rose. We knew she would be much more than her diagnosis. This is when we started our journey to fight for our girl, to be as prepared as possible, to talk to all the doctors, and to read as much as possible about what to expect.

I share those tough moments simply because it's

part of our story. It's a part of our story that I don't want to be a part of other peoples' stories. We need to change the narrative about Down syndrome and change how a diagnosis is delivered. It starts with empowering parents with the resources to connect with other people: social media accounts, local parent groups, support groups, etc.

Sydney Rose was born on March 14, 2020, just as the country was shutting down due to COVID. Becoming a first time mom was scary, the pandemic made it even worse. Do you know what wasn't scary? My baby. She smiled at us a few minutes after she was born and in that moment, through the happy tears, we knew everything was going to be okay.

I wish all the people who were involved in those appointments could meet Sydney. She's now 2 and a half years old and knows her letters, numbers and colors. She is smart, hard working and independent; she knows what she does and does not want. She loves music and she loves to dance. She has an infectious laugh and a beautiful smile that can melt hearts.

I wish they could see how she can make anyone and everyone around her smile. She can entertain a room full of people, do funny little things to make them laugh, and can truly make them happy. She has the innate ability to connect with people. My dad always calls her "magnetic" - it's almost hard to actually explain what this quality is, but it's certainly something special. People are just drawn to her.

Sydney has a little sister, Ryleigh, who is 17 months younger. They have become the ultimate dynamic duo, and are inseparable. We knew having a sibling close in age would help Sydney in so many ways, but we never imagined just how much it would help BOTH of them. Sydney is always worried about her sister, always making sure she has a snack, hugs and kisses her constantly and always wants to know where she is. Watching her blossom into this big sister role and seeing the love they have for each other has been one of the greatest joys of our lives.

To say that our family is proud of Sydney is an understatement. Our family has become closer and better in so many ways. We are so grateful for that extra chromosome and we're so grateful that she is ours and we are hers.

Everything will be okay. I promise.

Love,
Brianna Hamill

Meet Brianna

Brianna is a high school Physical Education teacher in Bergen County, New Jersey. She and her husband, James, have two beautiful daughters, Sydney (2) and Ryleigh (1), and they are expecting a baby boy this spring. Brianna is proud to be a Hope Advocate through Hope Story and loves to connect with families who have received a diagnosis. She loves being a part of the Down syndrome community and knows that Sydney is going to change the world. You can find her on Instagram @Breezybri66 or you can email her at Devereaux. Brianna@gmail.com.

LETTER 3
Extra Lucky Jessica F

Dear Mama,

If you are reading this letter, it's because you sit where I once did. It may be a different hospital room, doctor's office or your kitchen table but your mind is spinning. It's hard to catch your breath and your mind can barely comprehend what your ears just heard. Your baby has been given a diagnosis of…the name doesn't matter now, all that matters is your sweet little child. I can tell you this though, it's going to be alright. I hope reading this will ease your mind, comfort your heart and give you the peace of knowing life can still be absolutely wonderful, even with a diagnosis you didn't see coming. As mothers we have a choice, we can crumble into a puddle of despair (listen, a good cry does a world of good - just don't stay there) or choose to accept this new world, which I promise can be beautiful, amazing, fun, messy, crazy, sad, hard, fulfilling, rich and full of miracles and surprises. Life as you know it has changed, the life you imagined for your baby is different, but it's going to be alright. How, you ask? Everyone is different but hopefully you can take something from each story. Here's mine:

I have two children, Sophie (age 10) and her brother AJ (age 12). In May of 2018 Sophie had pneumonia, or so I was told. She was a pretty healthy kid but all of a sudden she looked awful. She had purple circles under her eyes, her belly was bloated, she was thin, tired and throwing up. My gut told me something wasn't right. After numerous visits to the pediatrician and being told "It's just another virus Mom, " I had it and demanded bloodwork. The doctor was very perplexed to see her liver enzymes were off the charts. I was sent to infectious disease, then gastroenterology, then cardiology, then rheumatology and neurology. It was a roller coaster ride of telling and re-telling her symptoms to specialists while she got sicker and sicker. I lived in New Jersey at the time and had access to all major NY/NJ children's hospitals and Philadelphia as well. We went to them all.

Finally, we thought we had a name for her illness: Necrotizing Myositis and autoimmune disease, causing severe muscle weakness requiring two years of immune-therapy and very high dose steroids. We began staying in a NY hospital five days a month and we had many ER visits in between. A few tips if you must spend time in hospitals: bring your own shampoo and soaps, pack comfy clothes, some games and even food you like and coffee pods in a cooler. A support person is great to have along too, I had my mom. She'd stay the night on a chair and I have to say as scared and tired as we were we never laughed harder. We used to decorate the room and IV pole. We had a lot of laughs in that stinky old hospital, it's how you get through it.

Sophie would respond to treatment then her labs would be crazy again. The more I researched (oh, you will become an expert on the human body when your child has something) the more I knew this wasn't it. Please, always listen to your gut. Take notes at appointments, keep a binder or file on your computer of test results and appointment summaries and question everything. If a doctor can't give the time you need to answer your questions, write them down and have their staff get you answers. You are an advocate now and no matter your medical knowledge you owe it to yourself and your child to become an expert on their diagnosis. No one knows your baby better than you. You will notice and see things that doctors don't, especially when visits are usually only 20 minutes long. It took one and a half years to find out Sophie had Limb Girdle Muscular

Dystrophy Type 2A/R1. We went from thinking she had a treatable disease to receiving the news that this is a progressive, muscle-wasting disease with no treatment or cure. When diagnosed in childhood, the chances of fast progression are much higher. I was told by one doctor Sophie would lose her ability to walk in two years. Well, she does gymnastics and cheers right now in fourth grade. She may not be as strong or fast but that smile and determination makes me tear up every time I see her. She also uses a wheelchair intermittently. She may need her chair permanently but there is no way of knowing when. We have good days and crappy days where she can't get out of bed or walk and so might you.

Sometimes she asks me why she has to have this. Those are hard nights and conversations with no good answers. There is no instruction manual on how to be a mom to a disabled child. You learn as you go, you read books like this, you connect with other moms online or in groups. But, the diagnosis doesn't define you or your child. I also have my son, AJ, and being a sibling can be hard too. Sharing yourself between your other children, doctors, therapy, work and other relationships can get tricky. Giving yourself some downtime, even if it's just ten minutes sitting in your car or mindlessly walking through a Homegoods store (that's my therapy) can do wonders. We need to be strong and put on a brave face and sometimes you just want to scream and cry, so do it in your car or wherever you can go get it out. Write a journal, just make sure you find a release for those feelings. I wish someone had told me earlier that it's ok to do all those things. I think I waited weeks to cry and then looked like a crazy lady freaking out in my car in a bookstore parking lot. Now, I do yoga. I'm far from good at it and my favorite part is savasana, which is basically just lying flat on your back on the floor at the end of class. I also have a gratitude app and every morning I type in what I'm grateful for. Sometimes it's easy, other days harder, but I always find plenty to write. On those bad days I can re-read what I wrote on other days and feel better.

I spoke at a conference recently that will be heard by the FDA to try and get approvals for therapies for my daughter, should they be discovered. Getting involved in your child's cause, once you get through the initial shock, can really help give you a sense of control and feeling you are doing something to help, just like I'm writing to you. I have dinner with friends, have taken a few short trips with my sister and have two jobs. I'm divorced, but have even managed to find a wonderful new relationship. I thought at one point I'd never see the outside of the hospital. Life doesn't end because of your child's diagnosis, it just changes and so will you. I was where you sit, although maybe different, still the same. Living presently is the best present to give yourself. Worrying can't change or fix things, so try not to let your mind wander to those dark, scary places. Enjoy your child's childhood now, don't spend it in the future. I told Sophie, we will always find a way to do what she would like. This might be riding an electric bike because her legs get tired or a beach cart to wheel her to the beach or a stool built by her Grandpa so she can play in her doll house easier. We just adapt and pivot. AJ, my son, has also had to accept and adapt. He helps her when she needs it but doesn't coddle her. They play and fight just like any typical siblings. He thinks of ways to help find his sister a cure and is wise beyond his years. He knows doctors and hospitals take me away from him, but rarely complains. This disease has taught him many things too.

I love my children to the moon and back and the words doom and gloom aren't in our vocabulary. We may have some storm clouds enter from time to time but the sun always comes out and it will for you too.

We moved to Sarasota, Florida because a warm flat

environment where Sophie can swim all year is best. Before her diagnosis I may have been hesitant to pick up and leave NJ, but you get very brave, which, I think, is a really good attribute to have. We have a handicap accessible house which we found already built this way - what are the odds of that? Who would have thought we would wind up living at the beach and who would have thought I would have a child with LGMD 2A/ R1? Life throws curve balls but it's not something to be missed. Whether you are sitting in that hospital, or in the sunshine, your mind can be a wonderful thing if you let it try and find peace. Our children are a gift and we are the lucky ones who get to be their moms.

It will get easier, your patience will increase, you will stop sweating the small stuff. What is a problem at work or stain on the couch when you have this under your belt? You got this, Mama!

Love,
Jessica Fabre, Sophie and AJ's Mommy

Meet Jessica F

Jessica is the mother of a 10-year-old little girl named Sophie who has Limb Girdle Muscular Dystrophy 2A/R1; A progressive muscle wasting disease. She is also mom to a 10 year old son AJ and a small dog Koko. They reside in sunny Sarasota, FL, previously from northern NJ. You can find her selling homes near the beach, working in her office or writing. They are surrounded by family and friends and live their life presently while continuing to fight for a cure for Sophie. https://www.facebook.com/jessica.fabre.359 and https://www.facebook.com/Heros-for-Muscular-Dystrophy-Calpainopathy-LGMD2ar1-105933000863866

LETTER 4
Extra Lucky Sarah J

Dear Mama,

I see you. I see your daily struggle, the sleepless nights, the endless medical bills, the worrying about your child's future. I also see your unwavering love for your child and the deep joy that raising a special kiddo brings to your heart and your home, despite the challenges, trials, and unknowns.

Many of us grow up with a vision of what our future will look like. We picture this perfect family with healthy, thriving children. When that vision is taken from us with a child's unexpected diagnosis, it can completely rock our world and break our hearts. But when your child with a disability has a small victory after months of therapy or they say I love you for the first time or you see their eyes light up every time they see something they love, that joy can make your heart almost burst. Mama, let that joy sustain you through the hard times.

My husband Jerrod and I struggled for 10 years to

have a baby. After several fertility treatments, we had our son Miles and we were over the moon. He was born 6 weeks early but is a healthy, thriving almost 10-year-old now. After Miles was born, we were told we would need to go back in for more fertility treatments to have another child. I prayed so hard for a sibling for Miles (for a baby girl specifically). After a couple years, we got pregnant again all on our own and I couldn't believe the miracle. Unfortunately, we lost the baby. The miscarriage was devastating, and I was almost sure we wouldn't have another miracle. A year after suffering that loss, we got pregnant with our rainbow baby, a baby girl.

During my pregnancy with her, routine genetic testing showed a very high risk of Trisomy 18; a rare condition that results in severe birth defects where unfortunately most babies do not survive past 18 months. I remember my OB telling me most parents choose to terminate with this diagnosis. I was shocked and scared but we were determined to love this baby as long as we had her on this earth; even if it was only 18 months. After several appointments, ultrasounds, and specialists, they couldn't find anything wrong with our baby girl. My doctor said that it was likely our daughter did not have trisomy 18 after all. However, he was concerned there was still something wrong because of the initial test results.

For every ultrasound I worried and every ultrasound she looked perfect. I went into labor on September 11th and I still worried that there may be something wrong with our sweet girl. My husband has the gift of faith and was my rock during this time (and always). He was confident our baby girl was going to be okay. And she was. She was born seemingly healthy, and we thought the tests were completely wrong. However, years of medical trials with many unanswered questions and several doctors and specialists followed.

We named our unicorn baby Macy which means "Gift of God" and "Warrior." We had no idea at the time how much of a gift and a warrior she would truly be. Macy was chronically sick from the beginning; starting with RSV at 2 months old, chronic respiratory issues, and 38 ear infections (and counting). We were told she just had "daycare-itis." She had feeding issues where she would choke as a baby and it was terrifying. We were told it was acid reflux and they put her on medication and a sleep wedge for months.. She had 5 surgeries before she was 6 years old including multiple hernia repairs and tonsils and adenoids removed to help with recurrent infections. She struggled with anesthesia and was often on oxygen for hours following surgery. She continued to get sick all the time and was on frequent breathing treatments. Her penguin nebulizer became her buddy. She started showing signs of speech delays early on, so we started speech therapy. She was starting to show learning delays and attention issues in preschool, so we began occupational therapy. She also demonstrated low muscle tone (hypotonia), sleep issues, bladder control issues, gross motor delays, delayed tooth eruption, and several dental issues. We also noticed a sensory sensitivity which made some of our day to day challenging; even things like brushing her hair brought on tears.

We continued to seek answers and felt there were so many pieces of the puzzle, but we couldn't find anyone that could put it together. I became an advocate overnight and never stopped fighting for answers. I found strength I didn't know I had. I asked to be referred to an immunologist and lab work showed she was immune compromised, but we still didn't understand why. I remember when she turned 18 months, I celebrated that milestone more than any. Knowing that my baby girl's life may have been that short never left my mind. Remembering that helped me truly appreciate the moments and milestones. Even though we had our challenges, I continue to have gratitude for her sweet presence in our family. She really does light up our lives and those around her.

When Macy was 5 years old, she started seeing a new speech therapist. I will be forever grateful for Meghan, her SLP, who noticed something in Macy and took the time to investigate it. At the end of her first visit, Meghan asked if I had a moment to see something. We went into the bathroom and she turned off the lights. I thought "what the heck kind of speech therapy is this?" She put a flashlight up to Macy's nose and had her open her mouth...and light glowed out of her palate. She told me she thought this was a submucosal cleft palate and was the cause of Macy's hypernasal speech and potentially her feeding/swallowing issues that she still has to this day.

I was in shock and my mind was racing. As a dental hygienist, how could I have missed this? How was it possible that 3 different ENT surgeons could have missed this? We were referred to a 4th ENT who specializes in cleft palate. While waiting for this appointment, I shared this update on social media. I have always felt if sharing Macy's story could help others, it makes the trials worth it. A friend saw my post and reached out to ask if we had done genetic testing; she had a patient in her office that day with Mosaic Trisomy 18. I suddenly flashed back to the genetic testing during my pregnancy and started researching if this was possible. Did my daughter indeed have trisomy 18 and she had made it to almost 6 years old?

The day we saw the 4th ENT was life changing. He confirmed the submucosal cleft palate with a fairly traumatic scope procedure. It is a "hidden" cleft palate so it is easy to miss but is considered a birth defect. He took one look at her and said he believed she has 22q11.2 Deletion Syndrome or 22q (also referred to as Velocardiofacialsyndrome (VCFS), and/or DiGeorge syndrome). He showed me some of her facial features that I always thought were adorable, like how her little ears stuck out (which was apparently due to missing cartilage). I had no idea what this diagnosis meant for our Macy girl or for our family but I cried the whole way home. A genetic blood test confirmed he was right. We got in to see the genetic specialist in our area who went over what all of this meant. 22q is a disorder caused by a small missing piece of the 22nd chromosome. This can affect every system in the human body and can be the cause of nearly 200 mild to serious health and developmental issues in children. It is oftentimes not diagnosed or recognized as the cause of a child's health and/or developmental issues for years. It is the second most common genetic disorder after Down syndrome, yet most have never heard of it!

I had a million questions. Some were answered and others would be answered after an echocardiogram, pediatric cardiology assessment, renal ultrasound, neck imaging, lots of blood work and another follow up with immunology. We knew we would have PT, OT, speech, extensive dental needs, ENT, and other specialists involved over the years to support her needs. I remember posting after this appointment "My brave girl did amazing today. This does not define her. It's what is different about her that makes her unique and special." I knew that despite this diagnosis, I would do everything I could to help her live her best life.

In many ways, it was a relief to finally have an answer. The diagnosis explained 6 years of health issues, developmental delays, and more. This also explained why her teeth had major hypomineralization and hypoplasia, meaning dental decay and infections were extremely common. Every time she had an abscess, or another tooth pulled, I felt like a failure. Shouldn't having a dental hygienist as a mom who spends so much time caring for her oral health prevent these issues? I struggle with the question "could I be doing more?" all the time.

On the other hand, the diagnosis was overwhelming. We had some good news that she did not show any signs of heart issues common in 22q and so far her kidneys are normal. However, we have no idea what the future holds. We will have regular echocardiograms, tests, and bloodwork to monitor her. Often heart issues and seizures develop in puberty as well as a range of other scary mental health issues common in 22q. I try not to worry about what the future will look like for her, if she will ever live on her own, or if she will choose to have children knowing that there is a 50% chance with each pregnancy she could pass this genetic disorder on.

I wondered of course if I had passed this onto her. I have some health issues and thought maybe I had 22q as well. When I got my test results back that I do not have it, I felt relief knowing I didn't have to add more appointments for me, and I could focus on caring for my little unicorn instead. The only reason I *kind of* wanted the test to be positive was to prove the genetic doctor wrong. When we were there for Macy's consult, she said she was sure I didn't have 22q because I had a Master's degree and am a dental hygienist. That broke c and I told her Macy wanted to be a doctor ne grows up. She said "that's not going to happen" right in front of Macy. I wanted to prove to her that even with a disability you can do anything. I just keep telling Macy girl "You are going to do great things my sweet girl. I believe in you."

Macy has spent much of her childhood being sick, on breathing treatments, having blood draws and medical tests, going to endless appointments, and having surgeries. She will need more surgeries in the future to repair perforations in her ears and her cleft palate. She has hearing aids, continued frequent infections, autism and inattentive ADHD related to 22q. She certainly has endured more challenges than most 7-year-olds can imagine. However, she is strong, brave and inspires me and those around her every day.

As a special needs mama, I lean on many resources for support. I joined as many Facebook groups I could find for her specific condition and special needs parents groups. I purchased books to learn more about 22q and parenting children with special needs. One of my favorite books is "Love and Logic: Parenting Children with Health Issues" by Foster Cline and Lisa Greene. I have been so encouraged by meeting other special needs moms in person or on social media. Knowing you are not alone and learning from and leaning on each other has been so helpful for me in navigating this journey.

I have also been incredibly touched by the amount of people out there with huge hearts for children with special needs. We have several local foundations I discovered that host incredible events for kiddos with special needs that have blessed our family tremendously. Macy was even nominated for a wish from our local Wishing Star Foundation and they sent our family to Disney World. Macy had a makeover at the *Bibbidi Bobbidi Boutique* and met the princesses. The joy on her face the entire week was absolutely priceless. Wishing Star even made sure her brother chose something special and he loved going to Harry Potter World at Universal Studios. This was a life changing experience and our family made memories to last a lifetime through all the trials we have yet to face.

This is the story of our Macy girl, our rainbow baby, and I wouldn't trade it for anything. She is kind, caring, extremely compassionate and empathetic, a great friend, she has the best giggle and makes everyone laugh, and she loves anything pink and sparkly. I am so thankful that God trusted us to be her parents. Our sweet Macy girl has made our lives so much brighter.

We share our story to encourage others, to share the hard times and the triumphs. To spread awareness and help other mamas know they are not alone. So remember, mama, you are not alone. You are strong, you are brave, and you are loved.

You've got this! With love,
Sarah Jackson, RDH, MS, Extra Lucky Mama to
#TheAdventuresofMacyGirl

Meet Sarah J

*Sarah is a mom of two little ones, a dental hygien-
ist, and a professor. She is a wellness advocate
and is passionate about fitness, self-care, mindset,
and living a healthy balanced lifestyle. Sarah is
the co-founder of Abundant Life Wellness Hub:
https://www.healthandwellnesshub.com/ ; FB:
https://m.facebook.com/100083104703926/ ; Instagram: abundant_life_wellness_hub*

LETTER 5
Extra Lucky Cara

Dear Mama,

I'd love to tell you about my very special daughter and the journey we've been on the past 5+ years. I want you to know that my daughter is the best thing that ever happened to me, but I also want to be honest with you. I didn't feel that way at first because fear and anxiety consumed me. I had to process, and get to know her, and learn to see past the fear. I wish that wasn't the case and I know it isn't that way for everyone, but in case you can relate, I want you to know that happiness did come.

My journey into disability motherhood started when I was pregnant with our third baby and the 20-week ultrasound raised some concerns. After many appointments and scans, we didn't have anything conclusive, only that our baby's fingers and toes were not visible in our ultrasounds. It was such a big thing, this unknown, that we carried for 20 weeks. It planted so many fears but also so much hope because so much

WAS healthy and strong with our baby. The strong baby in our ultrasounds is now five and all those things we saw as healthy are there and the differences we worried about are there too. But those differences don't make her any less loved and have taught us what we value as a family.

On July 4th, 2017, our daughter, Delaney, was born. If ever a child deserved fireworks on her birthday, it's her. Just as the ultrasounds suggested, she didn't have visible fingers or toes. They were there, just completely fused together. But everything else seemed to be okay. We even got to go home 24 hours after delivery, just like we did with her two older brothers. And while we were so happy to welcome a daughter to our family, I admit we had a cloud blocking our sunshine. The unknowns and fears were a lot to process, and we didn't have any immediate diagnoses. It also meant I didn't really know what to tell people if they asked or even how to share the news. I'm also an internal processor, so I needed time in my own head to make sense of it before I talked about it. Of course, our immediate family and friends knew, but we were pretty quiet about it – partly because we didn't really know what "it" was.

Four months later we finally made it down a path to a diagnosis from the genetic counselor in town (and if you are already navigating medical things, you know it was a windy road with persistence from Mom and Dad to make that happen). Delaney has Apert Syndrome. It's a rare craniofacial syndrome and a result of a mutation in the FGFR2 gene. It likely happened randomly in our case. I cried in the office when they told me. I was so sad to have her labeled with something other than "normal." But what I've come to realize is that the syndrome label is a blessing. I had something to research now. I could find other kids with Apert Syndrome and connect with parents like me. That opened so many doors for us as parents to advocate for Delaney and I know we're lucky for that.

Because I like making lists, I made a list for you of the five things I've learned so far.

1. Find your big picture and keep it in focus. Especially when kids are little, there is so much focus on hitting milestones. You see all the social media posts of proud parents sharing their child's first steps, first words, etc. and while milestones deserve to be celebrated, they aren't what truly matters. Delaney taught me to chill out about the stinking milestones. She largely hits them, but on her own timing. But that isn't

my point. My job as her mama is to raise her to be a happy, healthy adult one day and when I reflect on what that means, milestones aren't in the picture. It means that I want her to grow up to be a caring, helping, happy, loving adult. And you know, she's already bursting with love and joy at age five so we're doing something right. And I know I'll fight for her to keep that love and joy as she gets older. I want her light to shine bright and for her to feel fulfilled in life. We still work hard at all the milestones, but I won't beat myself up about them because I have the big picture as my North star.

2. Find the helpers and supporters. You will likely meet countless doctors, nurses, therapists, and medical professionals and some will be better than others. But if you look, you'll find some amazing supporters for your child(ren). That one nurse that takes an extra five minutes to get to know you and your child more. Or the therapist who asks you if you've ever considered that one preschool in town. The doctor that listens to all your questions and answers honestly. There are people with so much talent to share and they chose their professions to help others.

Find the ones that fit with you and your child. These are the people that I find myself thinking of in gratitude practice. When I reflect on the journey we've had so far, so many of the things that went well are because of these people.

3. Research. Early on there are so many appointments, and without a medical background myself, there was quite the learning curve. Luckily, I'm somewhat impatient and very curious so when I tried to get answers for my daughter's medical needs, I stumbled onto the path we landed on. We knew Delaney would need surgery on her hands and while they don't do it until 9+ months old, I wasn't going to wait that long to have a plan. A plan would ease my anxieties and help me see what our future looked like, so I needed to get answers sooner rather than later. And if I didn't like an answer, I didn't take it as an absolute. We ended up meeting with two hand surgeons and a foot surgeon in our hometown of Spokane and we weren't satisfied with the options. No surgeons here had experience with hands like Delaney's and they thought it would take 3-5 surgeries to give her fingers and couldn't tell us how many fingers they'd be able

to create. So, we drove across the state to one of the best children's hospitals for her syndrome to meet with a hand surgeon there. Similarly, they didn't have experience with her exact hand situation and didn't expect to give her ten fingers. So, we kept looking. It's a little silly to admit this but my most fruitful research came from Facebook. And it shows the power of connections with other disability families. I found my way to a few Facebook groups for Apert families and there was so much great information from people who have lived what we were just starting to figure out. I found the name of another doctor who specializes in syndromes like Delaney's. He's 1,800+ miles away from us but we scheduled a phone appointment and immediately found a doctor that could speak to our unique experiences and has intervention philosophies that felt just right for us. He operated on Delaney's hands and toes at 10 months of age and then again at 13 months and with those two surgeries, he was able to give her ten amazing fingers and 10 cute little toes. Then just two months later he operated on Delaney's skull (the first of a number of skull surgeries she'll need in her lifetime). So, we travel and it's expensive but I'm so glad we didn't accept any other options for her surgeries. We still meet with many specialists in our hometown but now we do so as empowered advocates. I wish I had realized this earlier, so I hope it helps you – you might be the only person who is looking at your child's entire lifetime of medical care across many specialists. Hopefully you have a great pediatrician like we do, because they'll help you too, but you ultimately need to feel good about your child's care. And if you don't, it's okay to push back or find other options.

4. Hold space for your trauma. This isn't an easy road. It's hard on our kids but it's also hard on the parents and people that love our extra special kids. When Delaney was six months old, she got very ill with RSV and had to be intubated and spent 28 days in the PICU. So much happened during that hospital stay that scarred my husband and I. My heart will never be the same after watching my daughter's life on the line. Somehow there was good in the experience – we witnessed what a fighter Delaney is, learned to appreciate a hospital, and gained perspective for

all the future medical needs. Maybe the biggest of all is how we were lifted up as a family. We were surrounded by prayers and support from family and friends, and the world started to see the magic of Delaney. This major life struggle opened the door for our network to see Delaney for the magical little girl she is and now we have all these people cheering her on and surrounding her with love. And yet, we still have PTSD from the experience. I don't think you can ever cure that, but I try to give myself grace when I feel the trauma coming to the surface. I find things that help me like exercise, sleep, gratitude practice, talking through things with my husband, and snuggling with my kids and/or dogs.

5. Embrace this life. I think this is where I struggled the most in the beginning. It took time to get to the point where I am now where I truly believe that Delaney is the best thing that ever happened to me. Everything felt SO HARD at first that I couldn't fathom surviving. Five years later and we're more than surviving. We're happy and Delaney is thriving. Life isn't meant to be all sunshine and rainbows and we gain a lot from the storms. Seeing how Delaney over-

comes so much adversity has taught me more about life and my life's purpose than anything else I've experienced in my 40 years of life. I hope you find this too.

I know our journeys will be very different but I hope some of the lessons I've learned can help you on your path. You've got this.

Love,
Cara

Meet Cara

Cara Hoag is a mother of three, Luca (9), Crosby (7), and Delaney (5). She calls Spokane, Washington home and works as a marketing director supporting enrollment at a public university. Cara and her husband, Matt, have been navigating the role of parenting a child with disabilities since their daughter's birth in 2017. Given Delaney's rare syndrome (Apert Syndrome), they found themselves becoming quick studies in the medical world and learned to ask questions, advocate, and embrace a difficult path to get the best outcomes for their daughter and family. You can connect with her on Instagram @ carahoag or email at carahoag@gmail.com.

LETTER 6
Extra Lucky Elena

Dear Mama,

Have you ever done a trust fall? Every school or corporate icebreaking activity I've ever been a part of seems to have involved a trust fall. You know, the one where two people are paired off and face the same direction, the person in front falling backward and the person in the back directed to catch their partner without letting them hit the ground.

When I think back on these trust falls, I don't remember much about being the catcher; that job needed to be done, so I did it. I only remember being the faller, and I can easily recall the many things I did wrong. I didn't always keep my body as stiff as instructed. I might have stumbled in that one scary moment where I lost faith in the person behind me. I might have shifted my arms for balance and made the catch more difficult than it could have been. I suppose not all falls were so poorly executed, but the good ones weren't particularly noteworthy.

In April 2017 at 10 weeks' gestation, we went for our second baby's nuchal translucency scan and were excited to find out if he or she could possibly have Down syndrome (DS) like our 15-month-old daughter. Although our daughter's Down syndrome is not hereditary, we'd grown fond of the idea of having a second with DS, where we would know which doctors to see, which therapies to schedule, even the best spoons and straws to introduce for feeding. What we weren't prepared for that day was that we would need to learn an entirely new disability, one which neither of us had any exposure to: limb difference.

Following the scan, the doctor told us that she couldn't find our baby's left arm. When my husband tells this story, he does it with a funny laugh and fantastically recounts, "Then look harder!" Yet we weren't so amused that day, and he didn't actually speak those words. Rather, we asked in desperation what this meant, but the doctor said she wasn't sure and that we should speak with a genetic counselor. Initially, I was opposed.

Two years earlier we faced pressure at this very same office to terminate our daughter based solely on a positive screening for Down syndrome and a related heart defect. Behind closed doors in the most vulnerable situation of my life, a hospital-employed genetic counselor looked me in the eyes and told me, "God gave us the ability to solve problems like these" as she weaponized my faith against our unborn baby girl. I was not interested in facing a conversation like that ever again.

But the fact remained that we did need to know what was going on with our son's arm in case there were implications to his birth plan. We were fortunate this time to be paired with a different genetic counselor, one who was honest, knowledgeable, and compassionate. We waited months for test results, and deep into my third trimester nothing had been revealed that would require immediate intervention.

Unlike my daughter who spent her first week in the NICU, my newborn son slept in a crib beside my hospital bed. After I had dozed off one afternoon during our three-night stay, he was taken from the room to have blood work done. With nobody nearby to stop me from finding him, I rolled sideways out of the bed, methodically dismounting without disrupting the internal sutures in my lower abdomen from my c-section. I shuffled my way down the hall, artwork on the walls fading in and out of focus, my head starting to buzz but my sights set on the room where my baby had been taken. I declined a wheelchair and sensed the warm presence of a nurse spotting me from behind.

During what was an arduous walk—realistically probably only about 30 feet—I worried that I wouldn't recognize my new baby when I saw him. After 9 months of pregnancy, I knew his kicks, his sleep cycles, the spicy foods that made him dance, but I didn't know his face. And there lying under a heat lamp was a newborn baby with one long right arm and one short left arm. His head was covered with the downy blonde fluff of a duckling. That was my baby. That was my Henry. I'd recognized him after all.

Every year we go to family summer camp, an incredible week-long getaway in Vermont where the kids have their programming, we can opt in and out of our own adult activities as we please, and we meet up in the afternoons for family fun. One of our favorite adult activities is the low ropes course, which involves a variety of low-risk adventures in the woods. One of these is a trust fall, but it's not like the obligatory ice breaking exercise we all know so well. Here, you have to climb up the side of a tree and fall backwards from a platform that's six feet high to land on the forearms of about a dozen adults waiting below, sort of like an organized mosh pit.

Having completed this same course four times now, I've seen and felt a lot. Each group is different year to year, bringing unique personalities and varying body types. We've caught trust-fall novices and experts alike. The ones who instinctively pike their hips when they land are tougher to catch, but we catch them. The ones who stay stiff but fall unevenly to one side require quick maneuvering from the group below, but we catch them. No matter whether a person is tall or short, the same group stands below, arms interlocked and ready to catch, and we catch them.

I don't personally love how it feels to fall. The vantage is quickly replaced by a pounding in my chest, realizing that I alone make the choice to shift my body back to a point of such vulnerability, which I would not be able to come back from on my own. I could stay on that platform alone, on display, growing more worked up the longer I hesitate, or I could allow myself to be guided into position and distribute my nerves to a community of men and women with outstretched arms below.

"3...2...1...FALL!"

I now realize that during a trust fall you don't fall

forward, seeing where you're going. You instead orient yourself as best as you can and trust the process.

If you recently received a diagnosis or have spent weeks or months wondering what this could mean for you, your family, and particularly your child, I will say this: Climb up that tree, face backward, close your eyes, and trust. Sometimes you will be the faller, sometimes you will be the catcher. Regardless of whether you have good form or not, your community will never let you hit the ground.

With love,
Elena Croy
Extra Lucky Mom to Hope and Henry

Meet Elena

Elena Croy is an ordinary mom learning life's lessons from her two extraordinary children. She and her husband are raising their little girl, who has Down syndrome, and their son, who was born with an upper limb difference, in northern New Jersey. Elena's disability advocacy, including community inclusion, has been featured on the Bergen County Moms channels. She chronicles her family's challenges, triumphs, and goofiness at AtHerOwnPace.com and on Instagram: @AtHerOwnPace.

LETTER 7

Extra Lucky Jaime

Dear Mama,

Diagnosis. I wish I could tell you I met it with open arms and "get it done" spirit, but that would be a lie.

When my son was diagnosed with autism spectrum disorder, at nearly five years old, it was almost as if you could see the claw marks on the walls of our life. They were mine, grasping at anything to avoid the inevitable. An undeniable truth was that the diagnosis was needed. Autism was there. It had always been there. It is currently here to stay. Forever.

Forever was the hardest part to swallow. Whether the diagnosis comes during pregnancy, at birth, or at four years old like it did for us, you don't just worry about tomorrow. You dwell on everything you used to think of as a given.

For me it was the sports, the family vacations, the first job, the high school graduation, and other typical life milestones. On a deeper level, I feared the relationship.

I only knew the stereotypes of autism and the idea of having a child who I couldn't build a relationship with broke me. It brought on tears when I thought about my husband not having the father-son relationship he always dreamed of. Worst of all, was the thought that my son may never know true love and friendship. Of course, I knew those relationships are not guaranteed in anyone's life but I felt as if it was now definite.

After dragging feet, waitlists, phone calls, an IEP in place at school, stacks of paperwork and an evaluation, we knew what was coming. Somehow, even with that knowledge in mind, the moment we were officially given the medical diagnosis, I sank inside. I was emailed a three page diagnosis and told a list of resources was coming. It never did. We were going to have to figure it all out on our own. That was daunting.

The day the diagnosis came happened to be two days after Christmas. I had plans to go see Little Women with my brother and sister. I cried the entire time and it had nothing to do with Jo or any of her sisters. I'm sure my siblings thought I was insane as I muffled my sobs for two hours straight.

Neither my son's life, nor my life, was going to be as I had imagined. I was dreading and worrying so much that I had to grieve the life I thought.

Oh Mama, did I grieve. If you are grieving, or fear doing so, please do without reservation. I didn't grieve my son; I grieved the expectations I'd had. Let yourself say goodbye to what never really was anyway. It will lead you to a clean slate of openness and acceptance of the unexpected.

It has been three years since my movie theater sob. No, those weren't the only tears shed, and there will be more, but I am in such a better place now.

In the beginning, so much is thrown at you. I immediately felt as if I had no instincts as a mother. All the outside advice chipped away at any motherly intuition that I thought I had. It didn't matter if it was the kind welcome advice that I sometimes asked for; the unsolicited advice I never wanted, or the advice from different sources that contradicted each other. All of it seemed to make me less sure of what I should do next.

While everyone else seemed to have predetermined paths built for their parenting journeys, I was, and am, on the path of the unknown. I have no choice but to forge that path into something just for my son. As an introverted and type b mom, I doubt myself everyday when it comes to advocating, but I will do my best to make space in this world for my kiddo. When you are ready, you will too.

What diagnosis really brought me was resources and support. I slowly took in opportunities. I took my son to a local day camp for disabled children during a school break. It was quite outside my comfort zone, but once there, I learned so much from other parents and the organization running the camp.

I also joined an online community. I know some people say your community is not online, but finding a group of parents who understood me, and what I was feeling, changed my life. Of course I have amazing family and friends in my life, but few understood or truly knew how I felt. Finding support without constant explanation brought me knowledge and s safe space to just be.

One of the best things I did was to start listening to disabled adults. I don't know where my son will be developmentally in a year, let alone as an adult, but finding adults who can give me an idea of what life may be like for him has molded my parenting. I have learned to let my son be who he is and embrace every part of him.

While it is still early for us, some of those worries I had in the beginning are transforming. My son already plays sports. No, he cannot participate on a typical team just yet. Instead, he plays Miracle League baseball and Top Soccer. Let me tell you, they are two of my favorite places to be. Seeing the joy it brings, to not only my son, but to all the individuals that participate, is a beauty I can't even explain.

We do go on family vacations. It takes preparation, modification, and I am often on high alert, but we make it work. We go slower and enjoy details that so many others might miss. We bond in our way and have found our groove as a family on trips.

The relationship I have with my son is nothing like what I feared. He is affectionate and sweet. He loves hugs and cuddles. He interacts best one-on-one with laughs and giggles. He and I have an unspoken communication that is necessary and unsurmounted.

He may not like to throw a football with dad, but he loves to wrestle, watch superhero movies and go to soccer matches with him. It's been amazing watching my husband make sure he modifies what he enjoys so my son can too. They are buds in their own way.

He has a little sister who he fights with like any sibling would. But she has also helped him grow so much and he has taught her the beauty of difference and compassion. She is always watching out for him. They are truly friends.

So yes, things are not what I had once imagined

or thought they would be, but that doesn't mean they aren't good. Now we have new dreams, new wishes, and new hopes.

The sadness still comes in waves. Sometimes I'll notice tears in my eyes as I watch the other kids at his school walking together and chatting away. Every so often, I have to walk away as I hear other moms talk about their children's piano lessons or great grades. Even at home, it takes me aback to watch my sweet daughter learn on her own through simple observation and practice.

These little moments will always happen. They poke at my heart every so often and I allow myself to be a little sad when they do. When they come for you, don't feel guilty. You are not alone.

My son has changed me and my life. I'm sad his life is hard and many times uncomfortable. I am always well aware our road is hard, but I am constantly working at finding the light and making his life better. You can do the same with your child.

Take it one day at a time. One moment at a time, if you need to. When the paperwork seems never ending, and the hope far off in the distance, reach out for help. Surround yourself with support. Find community in whichever way you can. Cry when it hurts and embrace the joy when it comes.

You've got this.

With all my love,
Jaime Ramos

Meet Jaime

Jaime Ramos is a wife and mom from Colorado. She's married to her best friend, Isaac, and they have two kids. Her oldest is seven and on the autism spectrum. She wants to spread the word that love and awareness is key to autism acceptance. Jaime is a blogger at Jaimeramoswrites.com, Facebook.com/jaimeramoswrites and Instagram. com/jaimeramoswrites. She is also a co-host on the Table for Five, No Reservations Podcast which you can find anywhere you listen to podcasts.

Letters 8-14

LETTER 8

Extra Lucky Amanda

Dear Mama,

I'm not sure where you are in your journey right now, but I do know the feeling you felt when you heard the words, "Your child has Down syndrome." I know those words made the room close in on you, and you probably felt like you couldn't breathe. Know that all of these feelings are perfectly okay. To me, it was so important to process it all. This isn't what you expected. You probably had a plan, a plan that didn't involve a Down syndrome diagnosis. I know you are frantically googling all things about Down syndrome, and you aren't finding the real-life stuff. You are finding the things "professionals" think they know about our precious children. But I am here to tell you mama, it is going to all be okay! This baby is about to open your eyes to a whole new world. You are about to experience a love you have never felt before. A joy that is unending, and a sweet, sweet soul is entering your life!

I know right now it feels scary. I know there are a

ton of unknowns, and you are unsure how to process the news or even move forward. I know that telling others seems like a task you do not wish to complete. You are worried about what others may think, or what your family and close friends may think of your new baby with an extra chromosome. Trust me, if they do not embrace this new baby with all that he or she is, you don't want them in your life anyway. They are the ones that will be missing out. You need a tribe that will build you and your baby up, cheering for you both and always in your corner. You'll need them on the hard days. Yes, there will be hard days, but hey isn't that what being a parent is like anyway? Does this life come with a little "extra"? Yes, yes it does. There will be extra appointments, extra therapies, probably some extra medications, and some things will feel so challenging. But it also comes with extra love!

The doctor is probably telling you all the health issues that people with Down syndrome can have. Or they may be telling you about how challenging life will be for them. To an extent they are right, but I promise it won't matter! When your baby begins meeting milestones on their own time, you will celebrate hard. Milestones will sometimes be discouraging. You will be doing everything you can to help your baby reach those, but they will in their own time. This was a struggle for me for the longest time, until I learned to let go of those expectations. You will learn to cherish every single thing they do, because it will be so special to you. You will probably have a few more health concerns to watch and monitor, but as I said before...it won't matter. You will do whatever it takes for them because they will be so worth it. They will face challenges in life, but hey, life is challenging. We all face them, and they will have the best momma by their side to help them along!

Our own personal journey was a doozy. My son's name is Colt, and he too is rockin' an extra chromosome. We didn't find out 100% that he had Down syndrome until after he was born, but I knew in my momma heart before. Colt likes to keep us on our toes. He was born at 26 weeks gestation, and only weighed 2 lbs. I knew the moment I saw his tiny body for a split second that he had Down syndrome. I didn't care though; I was too worried about his health. Colt had duodenal atresia, where his stomach and intestine didn't fully form together, so he was unable to swallow my amniotic fluid which caused preterm labor. However, he was so small they couldn't do his surgery to correct this until one and a half months later. So, our journey in the NICU began. It was hard; I'm not going to lie to you. It felt like some of the darkest days of my life. The NICU we were in was two hours away from our home and our family. We were commuting back and forth and every single time I left Colt, I felt like a terrible mom. It was grueling. Colt had his stomach surgery and a feeding tube placed at almost two months old. His recovery was rough, but once he was able to have some breast milk, he started making strides forward! He was able to come home after 105 days in the NICU. We came home on oxygen and a g-tube, but by that time I was just happy to be going home.

The worry set in once we got home. I remember setting his baby carrier on the counter and the tears started flowing down. How was this our life? How was this happening to us? Up until that point, we hadn't really shared with anyone except family and close friends about Colt's Down syndrome diagnosis. I couldn't even begin to process that because we were so wrapped up in his health concerns. When we got home and the dust began to settle, I began to process more. I felt a lot of grief. I was angry. I was sad. I felt it wasn't fair. Why us? Slowly I began to let go of those feelings. I began to celebrate the baby right in front of me. I began to realize what a miracle he was. I began to feel God knew exactly what He was doing giving Colt to us.

We spent a few months at home and Colt had to go back into the hospital for his open-heart surgery. He was born with an Atrioventricular Septal Defect, and we knew he would need surgery. I sure wasn't ready for that. I felt the fear creeping back in as I handed over my tiny baby to that surgeon. He made it out just fine, and after a few complications, and a pacemaker placement, we were home again, 31 days later. It was just in time for Christmas! I remember thinking this is all behind us now. We are on the other side, and hopefully we are on the uphill climb. We spent the next few months healing and learning to be parents to a medically fragile baby. Some days were filled with joy, and others weren't so much, and that's okay.

If I can tell you anything I have learned from parenting Colt, it is God is in control and I am not. Sometimes I have to learn to let go. I had to learn to stop predicting when things would happen...when Colt would reach this milestone, or when he would start doing x,y,z. I learned to stop focusing on the *what ifs* and remember the *what is*. I mourned the child I thought I was going to have, the birth experience I imagined, and accepted that life will look different now.

Not better or worse, just different. He is our greatest joy, and our biggest, unexpected blessing. Have there been extremely hard days? Yes. But mama, there have been so many good ones too. There are days where I rock Colt and thank God that he's mine.

Lastly, remember you are your child's biggest advocate. There will be doctors, teachers, everyday people that doubt what your little one can do, but you know their potential. Advocate hard for them and shout their worth through the rooftop. Shut down the misconceptions people think of Down syndrome. For a while you will be their voice, so don't be afraid to speak up because they will need you.

I promise it will be okay. It may not feel like it right this moment, but it will. Know you have a tribe of mommas behind you that are ready to help you! This community is a tight one. It's a community I never knew I needed, but so glad I have. The best days are coming! And hey...welcome to the lucky few!

With so much love!
Amanda

Meet Amanda

Amanda Schwiening is wife to her husband Josh, and momma to her extra lucky boy Colt, who is almost two years old. She currently works for a medical school in her hometown where she has lived her whole life. She loves spending time with family and her two dogs. They love going to the park, and spending time outdoors. Amanda loves sharing about their journey with Colt. Colt was born as a micro preemie and has been through open heart surgery. She loves to connect with her mommas on this journey and help spread awareness for the disability community. Instagram has been a wonderful place for her to share her thoughts, and process all they have been through. You can always connect with her on Instagram @a_schwien or by email akays2315@gmail.com.

LETTER 9

Extra Lucky Kelly

Dear Mama,

You just received the news, your baby will be born with Down syndrome, and at this precise moment, your world has turned upside down. The happiness and hopefulness you felt when you first found out you were pregnant has now been replaced by grief, anger, fear and confusion. You are probably questioning "how did this happen? Why me? This cannot be true." This might be the most broken and vulnerable you have ever been. I know mama, because just like you, I had all those feelings too.

The feelings you are feeling are valid. The future is scary, especially one that is unknown. I bet you have read and researched all Google had to say about your beautiful angel, and that scares you. You are now the most scared you've ever been. Yes, it is possible for your baby to have one of the many health issues listed on the internet, or NONE at all. Please mama, do not guide yourself with all these "possibilities." Again, it is just a *possibility*, it is NOT definite. You will soon learn that every baby is different, whether they have Down syndrome or not.

It took me a few weeks to finally accept and embrace the news. As terrible as it sounds, I did contemplate ending my pregnancy. I received that advice from many, including close family members. "It's going to be so difficult for you," they'd say, "you're young, you can try again," "If you're going to do it, do it now, you're right on time." You see, I was only 14 weeks pregnant and those were difficult words to hear; words that pierce the soul. Harder still was saying goodbye to a baby that I so desperately wanted for so many years. It took my then 9 year old to finally convince me that everything would be ok. As tears streamed down my face, my husband by my side, our daughter's response to her sister's diagnosis was, "Mommy why are you crying? The baby is ok, she's just going to be a little different. It doesn't mean we're not going to love her anyway." At that moment I knew that the thing I was most afraid of was the opinion others had about my baby because of her diagnosis. So I wiped away the tears, smiled and decided to continue with my pregnancy.

Now, one year later, knowing everything I know and experienced, I would still make the same decision.

I live for my baby girl's smiles, her laugh and celebrate every milestone.

The beginning of our journey together started a bit rocky. I needed to have an emergency c-section a day earlier because I developed gestational hypertension, uncontrolled. Together with my doctor we decided this was the safest choice for me and my baby. I only saw her for a few seconds before she was whisked away to the NICU because she developed respiratory distress syndrome (RDS) and started turning blue because of it. During her admission, an echocardiogram was done and we discovered she had a VSD, ASD and PDA which are congenital heart defects. I could not visit or be with her during her first days in the NICU, because I too ended up in the ICU after hemorrhaging a few hours after she was born. After 10 grueling days in the hospital, we were home, and my sweet baby girl was able to meet her big sister for the first time; and it was love at first sight. Little did I know that in just 5 weeks, she would become weaker, and she would stop eating. She would require heart failure medications, totaling to 8 different meds a day. This would necessitate a 2-week hospital stay that preceded a feeding tube. Finally at 3 months old, my little princess needed open heart surgery. This by far was the scariest moment of my life.

I found the strength I needed in God, my family, my friends, and in the beautiful Down syndrome community. Plugging into the community, via social media, DSAOM, and Gigi's Playhouse, helped me process everything I was going through, before and after, without judgment and with pure love. With my support system at hand, I was able to persevere through every single trial. My baby is now thriving and surpassing every milestone. She radiates joy everywhere she goes, and I cannot imagine a life without her. Now with the worst behind us, there is nowhere to go but forward, to our big and brighter future.

Once you hold your little one in your arms, and look into their beautiful almond shaped eyes, you will see the beautiful journey that lies ahead. Your experience may be different but know that you got this. As the song "Stand" by Rascal Flatts plays in the background,

"Cause when push comes to shove
You taste what you're made of
You might bend till you break
'Cause it's all you can take
On your knees you look up,
decide you've had enough,

you get mad, you get strong, wipe your hands, shake it off then YOU STAND"

You will realize YOU ARE ENOUGH. You are MOM, and it is through that knowledge that you will find the strength to continue with this journey, just as I have. You will learn to love and find happiness again.

So, Mama, go and prepare that beautiful nursery you envisioned. Plan that beautiful shower you dreamed of. Start making beautiful memories and begin to enjoy and celebrate your pregnancy. There is so much beauty that lies ahead. But most importantly, congratulations on your beautiful baby, and welcome to the Lucky Few >>>.

With Love,
Kelly

Meet Kelly

Kelly Caba is a mother of two beautiful girls, Brielle (11 years) and Abigail (1 year) and lives in Miami Florida where she resides with her husband and children. She works in a local hospital where she works as an ICU nurse and team leader. She connected to the Down syndrome community upon receipt of baby Abigail's diagnosis. Since then, she has begun to share her experiences and story to help other mothers who have received recent diagnosis. She would love to connect and talk to you. You can follow her story via Instagram @happy.abby.life or via email, kellcmar@gmail.com.

LETTER 10

Extra Lucky Michelle

Dear Mama,

Breathe in slowly…count to five…now breathe out. Count to five again. In these moments, take some time to simply just *be. Be and breathe.* Forget about the rest of the world. Repeat until you feel more relaxed than when you first started.

The truth is, we need to make sure not to just breathe, but to take care of ourselves. You may have just found out your child has a diagnosis. You may have always known. You may have a teenager who is disabled, or perhaps they are now in adulthood. Either way, we are all parents. We are moms, dads, and caretakers who are in the thick of it. It is important to take time to remember that before you were a parent, you were also an individual.

We signed up to be mamas, papas…we wanted the cuddles, the cute clothes, the firsts of everything, even the late night wake ups. But the surprise of a rare disease? Disability? Becoming an expert in genetics? Science? We did not sign up for this new world of medical appointments, therapies, and missed milestones.

When my daughter was diagnosed, officially, it was simply a formality. The truth...I knew from the very moment that I laid eyes on my baby girl after my cesarean that something just was not quite right. She was whisked away to the NICU and I did not see her for another 14 long, grueling, hours. In that time that moved oh so slowly, instead of glowing and loving on my new bundle of joy, I spent my time searching the web. *Down syndrome, Achondroplasia, Cerebral Palsy, and the list continued.* I compared what little I saw of her features in those two minutes to anything that would stick in my Google search. *Nothing quite did.*

I remember the feeling so well. My heart sank and this immediate feeling of gloom became apparent because I just knew. No one agreed or understood- even the most brilliant of minds. It took months of convincing my family and friends, even doctors, that there was a mystery to be solved.

As her mother, I pushed and pushed. But the day I received her diagnosis, it was just that. A formality- putting a name to her disability.

But when the doctor presented me with a packet of any information she could scrape together on this fairly new syndrome, *Jordan's Syndrome*, the words rolled off her tongue, and flew into one ear and out the other.

Less than 200 people diagnosed worldwide? Discovered about five years ago? What? How is this our life? How are we going to navigate this? How would we help her the best we could if there was so little information?

My husband and I were directed to a Facebook group. I reached out to the organizer, a fellow Jordan's mom and integral part of the team conducting ground-breaking research for our kiddos. I left her a message, expressing our new diagnosis and my fears. I prayed that this was not reality, and was hoping that when I woke up, it would be a distant dream.

I cried myself to sleep, weeping in my husband's open and comforting arms.

When I awoke, I noticed that my phone had about 100 notifications. I pinched myself to feel something besides the sinking pain that reverberated in my heart.

I scrolled through the messages that were sent from fellow parents who too, were walking the same path as us. We scrolled through the multitude of comments, pictures of their kids, welcoming messages of hope and love, continuing one after another. These families were sharing their stories, words of wisdom, but what really stuck with my husband and I were the pictures of these children, adolescents, and young adults.

These individuals resembled our Hailey. The similar facial features that I could not find while navigating the web; the stories compared to ours- the traumatic birth story, the NICU stay, the delays in her milestones. But the one feature that stood out, was the similar smile that spanned beyond her disability- the smile that showed just how happy she was knowing that her family loved her beyond measure and was doing whatever they could to give her the best possible life. So many of these children and teenagers, despite their difficulties and challenges, could be found with the same beautiful smile. And that is my favorite part about Hailey. Her smile.

Google could not provide that for us, but these people could. Finally, we felt like we found our people. Hailey, and the rest of our family, found a place to belong.

I am a believer in finding joy in our lives. We were dealt a really tough situation. It was not one that we expected. We did the routine genetic testing (all in which was "normal"), we prepared to become at first, a family of five, when Hailey was initially a twin. We grieved that loss early on. We then excitedly prepped our son for his new baby sister and for taking on the very important role of big brother.

But, truth be told, we did not prepare our son, our parents, our siblings, our friends, or ourselves, for the unknown. We grieved the life we had envisioned for us, but mostly, for our Hailey. We knew, we know, that her life will be full of joy, full of meaning, but it will be a hard road for her with an unpaved path.

But what we did not expect, the silver lining, was this amazing community that we now belonged to. It is funny, we spend our lives trying to fit in, blend in, be a part of something. We want so desperately to be accepted. Here we were, being a part of this totally exclusive, yet extremely inclusive, club. The rare disease one.

It felt so isolating, at first, thinking that there was no one else who knew the pain, confusion, and terror in not knowing what your child's future would look like. But then, you meet this virtual community who just exists. They share their battle stories, their successes, their tips, but mostly, they share their support that you didn't know you desperately needed.

I had my Jordan's Guardian Angels crew who literally knew my inner fears and our day to day life. But it became so much bigger than that. Parents of children with Down syndrome, Autism, various rare diseases, they became my shoulder. I leaned on them in the middle of the night when I needed to vent. They became a fundamental part of navigating this journey.

So mama...papa...whoever you are, wherever you are, just know, you are not alone. You have this community who is there for you. We may not be living the exact life you are, but we know. We understand, we empathize, and we see you.

There may be days when it feels just like it is too much- it feels all too overwhelming, or like you just cannot go on. Those days will not last forever. There will also be days when you forget your child is disabled, and you will smile at the small victories. You will smile along with them. Your heart will be happy. You will find that your child, while they may not be doing the same things their peers are or what you envisioned, you will realize that you are part of this bigger "thing."

You will experience what many will not. You will understand that life is not always easy, but when you laugh, a hearty laugh, or when you see your child doing something that took hard work and determination to get there, you will feel the utmost pride in your child and yourself for helping them get there.

But, aside from this community that will always be there for you, you need to be there for you, too. Breathe mama, you got this.

Love always,
Michelle, a fellow mama who loves you

Meet Michelle

Michelle Fruhschien is a wife and also mother to two children, Noah and Hailey. Her daughter was diagnosed with a rare genetic syndrome, Jordan's Syndrome. The moment they received her diagnosis, she made a promise to herself and family, to ensure that Hailey, along with the disabled community, would be seen, heard, understood, and included in society. You can find her @mamabear-forrare on Instagram, Facebook, Twitter, and Tik Tok. Her blog is located on her Instagram bio.

LETTER 11
Extra Lucky Sarah R

Dear Mama,

I write this to you as my perfect daughter is napping peacefully in her bed. She just had a physical therapy session where she worked so hard, determined to stand independently to keep up with her big brother. Myself? I'm juggling an ever-growing to-do list in my head, as one does with two toddlers that are taking the world by storm. My life wasn't always this busy, but it has been challenging in different ways.

This story is dark but I promise you there is a lot of light, too. Keep reading, mama, because this may be just what you need to hear.

I've had darkness following me much of my life; depression and anxiety are beasts that never really leave you and can be especially difficult to fight when the world is on fire. Such was the case in early 2020 when the pandemic shut everything down. I was in the throes of postpartum depression after a traumatic birth with our first. At the time of the lockdown, he was eight months old; we took him out of daycare and he was home with us every day as both my husband and I tried to navigate working from home full time. And then we found out we were expecting our second, unplanned baby. I was not okay. This was the worst possible timing considering we were in a global pandemic, our son was so young, and I was fighting my own mental health battles already. I felt so alone, so isolated with this news, and I couldn't see loved ones in person for the support I desperately needed. I felt no joy. Only despair.

At the ten-week-mark, I opted to get the non-invasive prenatal testing to find out the baby's gender hoping that it would help me to connect to the pregnancy. We already had a boy and, admittedly, I always dreamed of having a girl. At eleven weeks, I got a call from my OB's office and as soon as I heard the physician's voice, I knew something was wrong. We learned that day that our baby had an 84% chance of having Down syndrome.

To say we were upset by the results of the NIPT is an understatement. I sobbed. My husband researched. We googled (don't do this). I wasn't in the right place mentally to hear this news. I had never known anyone with Down syndrome and growing up I hadn't been exposed to people with disabilities. I was not prepared and I was terrified.

We decided to confirm with a diagnostic test, a chorionic villus sample (CVS) to be exact, which essentially biopsies the placenta via the cervix. The procedure was a bit painful, both physically and emotionally, but I had to know. It was this day that we heard the one and only "if you wish to continue with the pregnancy..." comment. At that moment, I was angry that it was positioned to me here, in the ultrasound room of the hospital just after we saw her on the monitor. There are better ways and much better places to have that discussion and frankly, these were not the people who should have brought up the topic. But to be honest, we did consider termination. My husband and I discussed it at length. Ultimately, we decided to move forward with the pregnancy. We had the means. We knew this baby would change how we see the world. We knew this baby would be a force, a humbling guidepost for our family, and be so incredibly loved by everyone around us. And so, we carried on.

I wish I could tell you that the decision to bring this child into the world helped me out of my depression, but it did not. I fell deeper into it. The remainder of my pregnancy was spent in a downward spiral of grief and "what ifs". My mind swirled almost daily with "why me?" Many friends and family encouraged me to reach out to people they knew that had children with Down syndrome or find online communities for support. I could not bring myself to do it. I felt deeply shameful that I wanted this baby but not the diagnosis. I pushed away books and other literature that was given to me, all from well-meaning loved ones, because it made it real and I wasn't ready to face it. I shared our news mid-pregnancy to close friends via email and asked for non-judgmental support as I navigated these dark and uncharted waters. I didn't know what was the right way to handle and share this news, but felt that everything I was doing was wrong. This only brought more shame and I continued to spiral.

My daughter's birth was about as rough as my pregnancy, with my water breaking spontaneously just before 35 weeks. She came fast and furious with the cord wrapped around her neck and twenty medical staff in the room. The nurse laid her on my chest as she was finally breathing through her cries. As soon as she heard my voice she stopped crying and looked me right in the eyes. She knew me, and I knew her…a little sliver of light to help me through.

We named her Halle, which has the Nordic meaning of 'heroine'. I didn't truly know then that she would be my hero–that she would save me by giving me a greater sense of purpose than I could have ever imagined. And here, begins the light.

Halle's first eight days were spent in NICU getting her oxygen and blood sugar controlled, with echos to check her heart and an overnight EEG to rule out seizure disorder. And finally, we brought her home. She was so tiny. But she was everything.

As the weeks went on, I began slowly acclimating to this new life. I once again found myself struggling with postpartum depression, so I joined a (virtual) new mom therapy group where I met others who have brought a new baby into the world during a pandemic. This was really helpful for me; I felt I was *seen* for the first time in a long time. To be able to seek help for myself was a good sign that things were going to be alright. I began collecting and caring for houseplants, which gives me a relaxing outlet when the world seems a bit too much. I also started to reach out to others in the Down syndrome community online and made connections that have helped me to navigate this new world of disability parenting. In hindsight, it would have been amazing to connect with these mamas earlier on in my pregnancy and Halle's life had I been in the right headspace. But this community wraps you in their arms no matter where you are in your journey! These mamas give me strength, hope, and a platform to share our ups and downs, celebrate our wins and grieve our losses. I am eternally grateful for having met so many amazing parents in the community.

Halle is a happy, goofy and determined little girl. Like many in the Down syndrome community, she has some medical and therapeutic complexities. Within the first two months of her life, Halle was diagnosed with severe obstructive sleep apnea and hearing loss. She has had three surgeries to support both, including numerous procedures to mend and open her complex airway and tubes for her ears. She is also in numerous therapies to help with fine and gross motor skills, including feeding therapy, PT and OT. She works hard at every therapy session, and she is learning both verbal and ASL words. I cry tears of joy when Halle accomplishes a skill she has been working so hard on. *This is the good stuff, the parts that shine the brightest.* The journey is challenging, but the celebration of all that this child can do, and will do, makes it worth the hard times. And I know, if she can do hard things, then so can I.

My true revival was when I began to advocate for Halle in medical, therapeutic and social settings. This purpose, almost primal, has saved me. I said earlier that growing up I had no exposure to people with disabilities. Frankly, I was afraid of them. How it pains me to write that now! That is not what I want for my daughter. I don't want anyone to be afraid of her because of her diagnosis and so, I advocate. More alike than different. Worthy. Capable. Deserving of respect, dignity and love. Shouting her worth from the rooftops.

To be able to look back and see how far I have come over the last few years gives me a sense of pride. I've come a long way from the new mama facing a disability diagnosis for her unborn child, battling depression and unable to cope with the world around her. To reflect on where I am today and greet the journey ahead with a smile is truly spectacular. There are days that I still struggle with the darkness but I am able to look back on all that Halle and I have done together and know that brighter days are within reach.

And so I am here, dear mama, to tell you that there is no right or wrong. If you are feeling grief, if you are depressed, if you are uncertain… it's okay to feel however you are feeling. This path has been paved in a multitude of ways by those who came before us. Some who feel joy. Some who feel sadness. Those who celebrate, and those who mourn. In the end, there is always light. This baby of yours will illuminate your world in ways you cannot fathom right now and I promise you that you will be okay. You got this, mama.

Forever your extra lucky sister,
Sarah

Meet Sarah R

Sarah Raphael is a mother of two, August (3) and Halle (2), and lives in southeast Michigan. She spent fifteen years in a corporate career, most recently as a Client Director at a tech consultancy. She has downshifted to focus on Halle's medical and therapeutic needs and her own mental health. Sarah is a fierce advocate of children with disabilities. She also loves yoga, reading, singing loudly (and proudly) and has more houseplants than she knows what to do with. You can connect with her on instagram @sarshieraph or email her at sarah-cwithers@gmail.com.

LETTER 12

Extra Lucky Erica

Dear Mama,

How are you feeling? How are you really feeling? What thoughts do you have swirling in your head? Now pause for a minute, write your feelings and thoughts down if you need to. Next, breathe and tell yourself that you will be okay. Your feelings and thoughts are all valid. It's okay to feel fear, grief, anxiety and depression. You are entering a new world of unknowns, challenges and surprises. "Why me?" "Can I handle this?" "What about my other children, my job, my life?" All these questions and concerns are perfectly normal to have.

Mama, know that I wish my words would be able to give you the peace and answers that you need. I wish that my words could help you see into your future and that you could see how much more amazing your life is about to get. Unfortunately, I know that my words can only go so far and that experiencing it yourself is the only way for you to find your peace. What I can do is tell you my story and what I wished I heard during those uncertain times.

My name is Erica, and I am a mom of two beautiful boys. Growing up I wasn't the girl that dreamed of careers and traveling. All I ever wanted was to be a mom. I was blessed with my oldest son five years into my marriage. Around the time my son was 3 we started planning for our second child, which led us to seek help through fertility intervention. I was excited to learn I was pregnant on my own, but soon miscarried around 12 weeks. We waited several years to process our loss and waited for a less stressful time to continue fertility treatments. After I graduated from my master's program, I decided to dedicate all my time to trying to get pregnant. We tried fertility treatments for several years but could not continue them due to the emotional and financial cost.

I longed for a second child but soon got to a place of acceptance with my one and only boy. My son was now turning 14 and we were gaining independence. I was happy and content. It was in that season of acceptance when I found out I was pregnant yet again. I was shocked, scared and extremely privileged to get to see a positive test again. At the 12 weeks scan the doctor told us about the first soft marker they noticed; that there could be an issue with the baby. I never heard of the Nuchal Translucency (NT) before then and honestly, I really didn't understand what the doctor was saying in that moment. I froze. After sharing the news with some friends, everyone kept telling me not to worry, nothing will come from it. After my blood work, I received a call to come into the office to review the blood work results. I went into a freeze mode again and all I heard was that my baby could have either Edward's Syndrome or Down syndrome.

We would need to see a genetic counselor to review the results further. The genetic counselor confirmed the Down syndrome diagnosis and ruled out Edward's Syndrome. Because Edward's syndrome is often fatal, we were relieved, but still completely ignorant of what a Down syndrome diagnosis would mean for us, the baby and our family. One thing that was certain was that we would continue with the pregnancy. The rest of the pregnancy was filled with fear for what could happen. I felt grief for what I may be losing. I felt frustrated because I wanted concrete answers. I felt guilty for feeling scared, like I was ungrateful. I examined each ultrasound looking for clues to confirm the possible diagnosis. I was so excited to meet my baby boy that when it was time for him to be born, I completely forgot that we would be confirming a diagnosis. My husband came up to me as I laid on the table and told me he thinks the baby has Down syndrome. I could not think of anything else but seeing him. I was only able to kiss him as they took him away. At that moment, nothing mattered, his diagnosis did not matter. I just wanted to see him, hold him, kiss him and soak all of it in.

When Noah was 2 days old, we reached out to early intervention and started the process to get him services. When we came home, we already had a handful of appointments. We did not know how his diagnosis would impact his health, so with each appointment we would brace ourselves for scary news. It all felt so overwhelming and surreal. It was also a time of gratitude and praise. It was a time to be grateful for his health and development. It was a time to slow down and prioritize our life. With Noah's appointments and therapies, we needed to shuffle our schedules around. We knew that we wanted Noah to experience life and all the fun that it can be. We traveled with him and maintained our friendships. It was tempting to stay in a bubble and close ourselves off from stares and perceived judgements. We went out, met other families that are extra blessed as well. We learned from them, felt supported by them and enjoyed seeing all the possibilities.

As I am on this wonderful journey, I am enjoying the lessons that I am learning along the way. I do not need to live in fear. We have survived 100 percent of our worst days and we know that we will get through whatever journey Noah's diagnosis takes us to. I am acknowledging that grief is part of this journey. Once I accept one part, I will get sad about another. I let myself feel it, validate myself and ground myself to the here and now. Sometimes this works, sometimes it takes more time and that's ok. I learned that I can not compare myself to any other parent out there. I have thoughts like "Wow, they do that for their child! How do they get all the strength, time, intelligence?" I question whether I should be doing those things too. Sometimes shame peaks its head up to spiral that conversation in my head. I learned that I do not need to jump in and be "Super Advocate MOM."

I am so grateful for the mothers that are fighting for our children, that are yelling their worth everywhere they go. I admire and aspire to be at that comfort level. I learned from them and have been bolder on social media and with people around me. I am still trying to figure out my place in advocacy. I know that living my best life and showing the world to Noah is a good place to start. Another lesson I learned is to protect myself. I need to know when to step away from information. There are very helpful social media groups out there that allow everyone to share the good and challenging areas of Down syndrome. I read a lot of the comments during Noah's first couple months of life, and I would cry reading about all the challenges. One phrase that we hear a lot is "do not compare," which in this moment means do not compare the good and the bad because Noah's situation will be different.

My story will not be your story, my experiences will not be yours. Our children will develop at their own pace and thrive in their own way. I also needed to protect myself from looking up every condition the doctors mentioned and abnormal lab work. I would try to interpret the result and sometimes bring more worry upon myself. I need to let the doctors do the explaining, not me. Understand though that you will know your child more than the doctors, evaluators and even therapists. You will be able to see them holistically so you may at times pick up what they may miss. I found that the first year I questioned everything and at times it did lead to him needing some type of intervention, but there were times that he was okay. Finding that balance is a challenge but it will come to all of us with time. My last lesson that seems the most difficult to apply is that I need to take care of myself. Being a special needs parent does not make me superhuman, I can burnout and find it more difficult to care for my family. It is not anyone else's responsibility to make sure that I have time to re-energize, take care of my health and my mental health. I need to be the one to ask for help when needed and make that time, and I do it because I love my family and I want to give them the best of me. Of course, it's easier said than done but I am a work in progress as we all are.

Mama, if anything, I hope that you can take away that our children are extraordinary. They will take us on a journey that is unique. You will get immeasurably more than what you wanted, needed and planned for. I say Noah is my surprise that just keeps surprising me every day. Your child will surprise you over and over again. It's a genuinely beautiful experience.

Many blessings on your new adventure,
Erica

Meet Erica

Erica is a born again Christian, an Associate Marriage and Family Counselor, wife to Marcelo for 20 years and mama to Nathan-15 and Noah-2 who introduced us into the Extra Lucky community. She loves spending time with her family and helping people find peace in their lives. Being in this community has helped her value life, hard work and self-care.

LETTER 13

Extra Lucky Ashley

Dear Mama,

> "Even when God doesn't perform the miracle in the way we have prayed, He is still the God of miracles, and there is still a miracle that has been performed.... We just need to ask Him to open our eyes to see how He has decided to perform that miracle."
>
> —*anonymous.*

I remember the day I saw this quote posted on Instagram and I knew in my heart that it was meant for me as if it was sent in my path by God Himself. You see, my 3rd pregnancy was filled with extra doctor appointments, extra worries, extra fears and an extra chromosome that wasn't definitive yet but would soon fill my heart with extraordinary love.

From the start of this pregnancy, something felt different. I remember going to that first appointment around 9 weeks, hoping and praying I would hear a heartbeat and the baby would measure well. Sure enough, everything looked great. But that uneasy feeling lingered inside me which turned out to be my very real motherly instinct. You will have it too, if you don't already, and it will guide you through this life.

As the 12-week scan approached I had this overwhelming feeling that something would be wrong. Oddly, the morning of my scan, my total at the gas station was $50.50, a number that made me feel uneasy for some reason and would have great significance later that day. Sure enough, during the sonogram, the perinatologist found a large cystic hygroma (fluid filled sac) behind the baby's neck while measuring the nuchal fold. And in a stoic voice she said this indicated a 50/50 chance of a genetic syndrome like Down syndrome or the chance the baby may not survive if the fluid did not resolve before 20 weeks gestation. When she began to mention next steps and the options, I quickly stopped her and said I would be carrying this baby to term or however long God intended. My husband Anthony and I also decided not to do genetic testing because we were fully accepting of whoever this baby was going to be, though fear still lingered, as the unknown can be quite scary. And there it was, the thought I feared, the one buried deep inside me from the start. I said to myself *this can't be happening, why is this happening? What about the boys? How will I get through this?* But it did happen, the reason was great. Angelo and Matthew are oh so lucky and I got through it with flying colors. So will you Mama, I'm sure of it.

The following weeks were filled with lots of prayers, follow up appointments, an early anatomy scan and a change in OB/GYN practices after having yet another disheartening conversation with my current doctor. I couldn't help but get the feeling that she wanted us to terminate the pregnancy based on the possibility that this baby wasn't "perfectly healthy" by medical standards and by possibly not being so their life wasn't worth living. I knew I couldn't spend the next 6 months with her. So, we found a new high-risk Dr. at a new practice, and I began seeing her around 18 weeks and that was when things started to change. She approached me so caringly during the first appointment and wanted to take a look at the baby and take some of her own measurements which looked perfect and the cystic hygroma was nearly gone. However, a second anatomy scan around 20 weeks revealed an initial concern regarding the baby's heart, which required follow up echocardiograms with a pediatric cardiologist for the remainder of my pregnancy. This made me more nervous than a possible Down syndrome diagnosis. Yet, from that point on the pregnancy was unremarkable as the baby continued to grow well, no other soft markers typically seen in fetuses with Down syndrome or any other genetic condition were noted, the "heart concern" (aortic coarctation) remained stable and was even thought to end up being a normal occurrence once she was born.

Fast forward to 38 weeks pregnant and the call that changed everything. The cardiologist called to follow up on the latest echocardiogram. She explained that not only did the latest scan show the original possibility of coarctation, which wasn't a concern, but possibly two holes and a mitral valve cleft. She continued to say that this heart condition is known as Atrioventricular Septal Defect, and it is the most common congenital heart defect found in children with Down syndrome. She said that since the baby had a cystic hygroma there was a greater likelihood that the baby did in fact have Trisomy 21. She then said, this would require open heart surgery and I could feel life draining from me. Talk about the shock of your life. That miracle I prayed so hard for and believed in was instantly gone. When I think back on that day, I wish I knew what I know now. I wish I trusted in God's will for us, for our family, and for the miracle that He would place in my arms just a short week later.

On June 3, 2020, in a New York City hospital I gave birth to the baby girl I dreamed about my entire life. She was finally here, she was perfect, I loved her with every ounce of my soul, and she had Down syndrome. We named her Cecilia Lee after my grandmother and St. Cecilia. And at that moment every fear I had for the last 9 months had instantly gone away and I felt completely at peace. I was exactly where I was meant to be, and my daughter was exactly who she was meant to be. The hours following Cecilia's birth seemed endless as she was being monitored in the NICU. I remember being wheeled down to see her by a nurse and the NICU Dr. came beside and congratulated me on my new beautiful little girl. I felt surprised, I didn't expect it, I thought an *I'm sorry* was coming and it never did. I said "thank you" and my next words were "I know she has Down syndrome and that's ok, I love her so much and I'm proud to be her mom." He responded with, "I have a cousin with Down syndrome, and he is awesome, he has a great life, he is loved, and he loves who he is. Cecilia will have a great life, she will change yours, you are so lucky to have her." I wish I thanked him for his words, but I just smiled. I smiled because of his kindness in the realm of so many unknowns, I smiled because he was right, I did feel lucky, I felt blessed, I felt God had given me a tremendous gift.

So here I am two years into this extra lucky journey with an incredible little girl who has taught me more about the power of God in her short life than I have known in my 36 years on this Earth. She survived open heart surgery and is thriving. She has determination and resilience I didn't think was possible for a two-year-old. She has reached so many milestones and continues to surprise us every day with a new sign, new word, new skill and new curiosity. She waves to say hi to everyone and anyone in her path and always receives a smile back, a kind hello and an added compliment of how friendly she is. She makes people happy and draws them into her world even for just a moment. She gives the very best hugs, kisses you just because and when you say, "I love you", has learned to bless herself with the sign of the cross and has the very best bond with her brothers. She is adored by her family and our closest friends, and I thank God every single day for her. So, Mama, if you're worried what your child's life will be like or how different yours will be just think of my story and Cecilia and know you are blessed to be part of this extra lucky life.

With all my love,
Ashley

Meet Ashley

*Ashley DiPietro was born and raised in West-
chester, NY where she resides with her husband
Anthony and their 3 children Angelo (6) Matthew
(5) and Cecilia (2). She is currently a stay-at-
home mom but has a Master of Science Degree in
Speech Language Pathology. She is of the Catholic
faith and believes in the Right to Life. She began
connecting with many lucky few and heart mamas
shortly after Cecilia's birth through Instagram. She
would love to connect with you to answer questions, listen to concerns, give advice and put your
heart at ease after receiving a Down syndrome
diagnosis. She can be reached via email at ash-
leym621@hotmail.com or through her Instagram
account: ashd324.*

Extra Lucky Elizabeth

Dear Reader, the letter below is an incredibly honest story of a mama's struggle with acceptance of her child's diagnosis, and their journey with a complex, rare heart defect. We wanted to let you know that it also deals with child loss. We are beyond grateful to Elizabeth for sharing her story, as we know the feelings within will help many mamas feel seen. However, if you feel that you are not ready to read a story that contains loss, we recommend coming back to this beautiful letter at another time.

Dear Mama,

There are so many things about this journey that are pure joy. The anticipation leading to meeting your baby, actually meeting them, and every milestone and inchstone between those milestones will bring you more warm fuzzies, excitement, and pride than anything you've ever experienced. Every accomplishment is amplified because it does not come easy.

My husband and I had a different experience than most with our son, Barrett. We found out that he had a complex heart condition at my 8am anatomy scan at 18 weeks. My maternal-fetal medicine (MFM) doctor could not visualize Barrett's left ventricle, the chamber of the heart that pumps oxygenated blood to the rest of the body. He was able to get us in with a pediatric cardiologist that day, and by 5 p.m., we had a confirmed diagnosis of Hypoplastic Left Heart Syndrome (HLHS). We made an appointment to come back in a month with the understanding that we would begin meeting with staff at the local children's hospital and start putting a birth plan together, as I would have to deliver at a different hospital.

The week before, my MFM had seen a couple of soft markers for Down syndrome – shortened nasal bone, thickened nuchal fold, and a short femur – so he sent me to my OB's office for a blood draw. The NIPT results came back the day after we received Barrett's HLHS diagnosis. Barrett had a 47% chance of having Down syndrome based on that blood draw. We immediately scheduled an amniocentesis to ensure we had as much information about Barrett as we could. Two weeks later, it was confirmed that Barrett had Down syndrome.

I'm not going to lie – Barrett's Down syndrome diagnosis hit me like a ton of bricks. Almost three years after our prenatal diagnosis, I am still not sure that I have entirely processed it. It would be entirely dishonest for me to say that I felt lucky to have a child with Down syndrome. When we received Barrett's heart diagnosis, I cried for two days and then started figuring out how we would make it. The traditional treatment for the diagnosis we had received at this point involved a series of three open heart surgeries. Ideally, the first would be within the week of birth, the second at about 4-6 months old, and the third sometime between 2 and 4 years old. I felt like we were about to embark on a five-year heart journey and that after that third surgery, Barrett would have a relatively "normal" childhood (yes – I was so naïve. Does normal even exist these days?!). His heart was something that required immediate attention, so most questions I had regarding his Down syndrome diagnosis were kind of on the backburner while I was pregnant.

The Down syndrome diagnosis for me was much harder than the heart diagnosis because I never felt like there was the proverbial "light at the end of the tunnel." As a first-time mom, I had just made peace with the idea that we were going to have to change our lifestyle for the first five-ish years of Barrett's life due to his heart surgeries, and then I was told our son had Down syndrome. We were told that "we had options" regarding this pregnancy, but we didn't consider anything other than raising our son. I mourned the loss of normalcy – the dream that he would be valedictorian of his senior class, have a college experience like his father and I had, have a career and a family. Now, I recognize that so many of those things are possible even though they may look a little different, but then, I just could not see it. The magnitude of being responsible for my son as an adult in ways that the majority of mothers do not hit me hard. I ached for the same parenting journey as my friends and my sister, who had neurotypical children with no heart defects. Now, two and a half years later, I still feel like this was the hardest part of Barrett's big adventure – his mother coming to terms with his Down syndrome diagnosis. As controversial as it may sound, I have never felt that I was given a gift with that third copy of his 21st chromosome.

I tell you this ugly part of my story because I wish someone would have told me that it was okay to not feel like it was all rainbows and sunshine without pitying me. The most well-meaning people without a child with extra needs would say things like "special people are chosen for special babies," and it would send me into an inner tailspin. I really felt like no one knew how I felt because my son wasn't just a heart baby or a kid with Down syndrome – he had a heart defect that was so rare when combined with Down syndrome that I had a hard time finding mamas with kids with DS/HLHS. At my lowest points, I didn't even feel like I could connect with the moms who had babies with heart conditions and DS because the majority of their kids had "typical" defects for a person with DS. Looking back, I wish I would have talked with a mental health professional because I felt so much guilt for not feeling like I belonged and having such uncomfortable feelings with Barrett's Down syndrome diagnosis. I truly think it was so hard for me to come to terms with it because no one can truly tell you what your child with Down syndrome can achieve. Once I stopped seeing his diagnosis not as a limitation or a set of expectations, it was almost empowering for me. I tried to see the DS diagnosis as things that could be the case, but not always things that would apply to my son.

Once I made peace with how we would approach his Down syndrome diagnosis, it started to hurt even more when others limited him based on the label and expectations they had for a child with Down syndrome. Remember how we were making plans with the children's hospital and the pediatric cardiologist regarding Barrett's treatment plan? The week of our second appointment, I had been messaging with the nurse practitioner about a few things and mentioned that the amnio results confirmed that Barrett had Down syndrome. She was typically quick to reply to my messages, so when I didn't get a response within 24 hours, I was feeling a bit uneasy. Our appointment was a couple of days later, so I tried to tell myself that she would touch base with me at the appointment.

We arrived for the appointment and had our normal echocardiogram. The cardiologist came in afterwards and confirmed that he was still seeing the same things that made him diagnose Barrett with HLHS. The conversation then took a turn when he mentioned that he was told the amnio came back positive for Down syndrome. He told us that he had spoken with the heart surgery team at the children's hospital, and they did not feel Barrett was a candidate for the originally planned surgery. The reason we were given was that babies born with Down syndrome are at a high risk for increased pressures in the lungs, and for the first surgery, pulmonary pressures need to be low. The cardiologist told us that we had three options for Barrett's care: to proceed with the original plan and hope that his pressures were low and the heart surgeons changed their mind after he was born, find another surgical team, or place him on "comfort care" after birth and forgo any surgical interventions. This was the second time we were given the option for our child to die and to say it devastated my husband and I is an understatement. We immediately said no to option three and asked the cardiologist if there were any programs he thought would consider our case. He recommended we go to Boston Children's Hospital, but ultimately sent our case to the other five programs in the state he was aware of and one in the neighboring state where we would be close to family. All of them but one said they would not take our case, and the other never responded. In a matter of days, we went from handling everything roughly an hour from our house to potentially moving across the country for the better part of a year. We were devastated – two of those programs were ranked incredibly high in the US News and World Report rankings for pediatric cardiology programs the year before.

We are of the Christian faith and feel like what happened next could only be described as a "God thing." A friend of my family reached out after I had posted an update on our pregnancy on social media and shared that she and her husband, a general surgeon, had connected with the chief of the Children's Heart Institute at Children's Memorial Hermann Hospital in Houston, Texas through a medical missions event at their church. As I understand it, they were at the same table at this event and Dr. Jorge Salazar was sharing about his work with children with Hypoplastic Left Heart Syndrome. Her husband reached out to him and asked if we could contact him, and after a phone call that evening, we were heading to Houston. Barrett's Down syndrome diagnosis was used to "inform decisions," but was never something that our team at Hermann used to justify a decision unless it was based in research. His pulmonary pressures were closely monitored, but never an issue for his surgeries. After Barrett was born, his official diagnosis changed from what was initially considered HLHS to a broader, single ventricle diagnosis of an unbalanced, right dominant AV canal defect with a hypoplastic aortic arch. Instead of treating his heart condition through the textbook three surgery path, which would be risky and wouldn't be sustainable for him long-term, Barrett had a band placed on his pulmonary artery to limit blood flow to his lungs. This made it possible to manage his heart failure until he had grown enough for a Bidirectional Glenn procedure at 4 months. He then was going down a path for a biventricular repair – something that was never mentioned at our original hospital. The expectation after that bivent was that Barrett would use both ventricles – his whole heart – rather than just the right ventricle, as would be the case with the standard course of treatment that was originally considered for him.

Our team at Children's Memorial Hermann was willing to think outside the box when it came to our son, and that truly helped shape how my husband and I began to parent our son. Because they showed us from a medical perspective how to create opportunities for him to succeed, we became more confident in advocating for him and creating opportunities for success in his everyday life. We will forever be thankful for our team for giving us the space to grow as Barrett's biggest advocates.

We will never know how the story with his heart would have played out. Barrett passed away suddenly at 23 months old from a hemorrhage five days after a routine tonsillectomy. It is an incredibly rare risk, but one that we encountered. Before his death, we were able to experience the greatest joys of parenting a child with extra needs – the inchstones. Trust me, when they hit the major milestones, it's a cause for celebration, but so is when they hit the inchstones in between. When

Barrett held his pacifier in his mouth, lifted his head during tummy time, passed a toy from his right to left hand, brought food from his tray to his mouth – these were all moments that brought just as much joy as his rolling over or sitting independently. Our son was pure joy – not because of his diagnoses or his challenges, but because he was Barrett. Everything was amplified because of the challenges, but at the end of the day, all children have challenges and labels placed on them. Down syndrome was one label Barrett was given and his heart defect was one challenge he faced, but ultimately, the fact that he was our son, and our relationship was like that of any heart healthy, neurotypical child and their parents.

Mama, what I hope for you is the same as what I hope for the mama of any other child – that you can find joy in the hardest of times. I know what it feels like to wish your life was different. It is absolutely okay to feel that way, but to be able to find joy and peace in the life you're living – especially when facing challenges that very few around you are – is the best gift you can give yourself and your child.

Cheering you on,
Elizabeth Rhyne

Meet Elizabeth

Elizabeth Rhyne is the mama to Barrett and wife to Robert. Barrett passed away on April 27, 2022, at 23 months old, but had quite a life in those 23 months. His story can be found on Facebook by searching "Barrett's Big Adventure." Elizabeth holds two degrees from the University of Oklahoma. She and Robert now reside in Oklahoma and enjoy finding new favorite restaurants, spending time with family, and binging true crime documentaries and podcasts. Her Instagram handle is @earhyne.

Letters 15-21

Extra Lucky Colleen

Dear Mama,

Chances are, if you are reading this, your life has just been overturned by your child's diagnosis and you are searching for someone to relate to. This is where I was just a few years ago. None of the stories I read in my preparations felt like they matched our family, they were either incredibly religious or written by extroverts. Nothing I read matched how I felt, in fact many stories made my emotions feel wrong. Recently, a few wise women in my life have focused on the validity of ALL emotions and the role they play in life's big moments. I hope as I share the array of emotions felt in our diagnosis journey that you can see the unfiltered beauty of becoming an extra lucky mama in the light and dark times.

Apprehension:
We don't have an official diagnosis day.   Due to anxiety and a family history of high-risk pregnancies, my husband and I elected for the 12-week quad screen;

we never thought we would be receiving a phone call that our labs came back abnormal. My provider was kind, thorough and wonderful but I don't remember exactly what she said or what I said when I called my husband to share the news that our wonderful baby showed an increased chance of having Trisomy 21, otherwise known as Down syndrome. After I hung up, I remember crying in an eerily empty hospital hallway, thanks to the beginning of the pandemic, then returning to work.

Our genetics consultation to review our testing results was conducted virtually via telehealth, again because of the pandemic. It was surreal to conduct a life changing appointment through a computer screen. We learned that the likelihood of T21 had now increased to nearly 90 percent. In my heart, despite the high likelihood from NIPT, I held out a hope she didn't have it. We kept our diagnosis quiet, electing only to share with close friends and family just in case it was wrong.

Though not a confirmed diagnosis our pregnancy was treated as though our daughter had T21. This included a slew of extra ultrasounds, cardiac echocardiograms (ECHO) and fetal monitoring. A fetal ECHO showed a spot on her heart, We surged from 90% to

99%, but then our fear shifted from the adversity our child may face to our sweet baby needing heart surgery.

Loneliness:

The remainder of my pregnancy felt like an eternity; I was consumed with researching everything I could, checking on my baby and being "prepared" for all the what ifs. Thankfully, we didn't have any more prenatal diagnoses to add to our concerns. My relationships with friends I deemed close had shifted, it felt like some were in denial, acting like I was ridiculous for expecting a NICU stay, while others expressed concern but conveyed pity. I forged relationships with the ladies in my centered pregnancy appt, and though accepting, none of them completely understood. Keeping the diagnosis a secret felt like I was living a double life; acquaintances expected us to exude excitement for our little girl, in reality we were both fearful of the future. In my research I began following social media accounts, connected with The Down Syndrome Diagnosis Network (DSDN) and local DS organizations. It felt like a breath of fresh air to have these new virtual friends and not feel alone as we waited for so much unknown. These virtual friends shared our fears, provided support and celebrated the achievements of people with Down syndrome. Finding our people, *the lucky few*, rekindled excitement for her arrival.

Shock:

On September 17th, at 36 weeks, we didn't pass the fetal wellbeing exam. The growth scan showed that I had lost most of my amniotic fluid and her heart rate and breathing were not right. When the fetal medicine doctor shared this news and told me I would be admitted for induction, my body went into autopilot. I called my husband to make arrangements, then drove to my son's daycare to hold him, not knowing how long I'd be away. We hurried to the hospital, got hooked up to monitors and then waited an excruciating 48 hours for the steroid shot to help mature the baby's lungs to take effect. The induction began smoothly, and I got my epidural a few hours in. Suddenly the whole team rushed in; the baby wasn't tolerating the induction and we needed to pursue a cesarean section. Even though this was one of the possibilities I had prepared for, the reality of it was daunting. I signed the paperwork while my husband Dustin updated our family. The team came back prepared for surgery and ran me down the hall to the operating room. My body shook as they transferred me to the operating table and the anesthesiologist asked if I was going to be sick. Next thing I know the doctor was holding up our daughter, Amelia. I was in shock, all I could acknowledge was, that's our baby.

"Come on cry" I heard my husband beg and cold realization crept in; Amelia was quiet and gray. She was taken to the resuscitation room, then down to the NICU, accompanied by my husband because I didn't want her to be alone. Once stabilized, I was wheeled down to see her myself. I was able to hold her for about 2 minutes, then they took her to intubate.

The next two days were a blur, she was unstable and battling pulmonary hypertension along with the cardiac issues and prematurity. We could not talk to her or touch her because she needed a low sensory environment, but we were allowed to do cares.

On her third day of life, she had decompensated so much that the team interrupted rounds to see her. Her pulmonary pressure was continually rising and approaching the threshold for ECMO. She would be transferred to a level 4 NICU that was capable of this intervention and she would be flown. No amount of planning prepared us for this.

My doctor had been texting me, knowing Amelia was critical and she came to discharge me early so I could be with her at the other hospital. We rushed home to hug our son and pack essentials and then we embarked on the longest 2 hour drive of our lives. We arrived emotionally exhausted and were escorted to the NICU only to discover that we had beaten the helicopter. Bewildered by this, we were left waiting for 2 agonizing hours before we could see her and know she was "ok." The ECMO equipment was in the hallway on standby and she had two IV poles laden with IV's. Our birth story felt like a medical drama, not real life.

Joy:

After a torturous week, Amelia was ready to be extubated. We finally got to hold our feisty little fighter. She finally felt real, and I was able to have a "normal" mom experience. She continued improving and our concern shifted to how we would juggle having our kids 2 hours apart. Since she was stable, we worked our way up to an overnight at home with our son. As we were loading up the car to return to Amelia, my phone rang. We were told not to come back; transport had been arranged and Amelia would meet us at our local NICU. My eyes flooded with relief and gratitude. Because of the benevolence of the NICU that absolved the cost of transporting her back, juggling kids in two places felt manageable. Having her at "home" may have been more exhilarating than her traumatic birth.

Impatience:

We expected once stable, Amelia would grow a bit more then come home until her heart surgery. Instead, we spent 9 weeks dividing our days between work, the hospital and home because she would not be stable at home. Amelia's first Halloween, Thanksgiving, and Christmas were spent in the NICU. Due to COVID exposure, we missed her first Halloween altogether and were isolated from her for a heartbreaking 10 days. Then, we became regulars in the unit. Amelia was assigned the most amazing primary care nurses, we met another lucky family with whom we bonded over G-tube placement, looming cardiac repair and a love of bows. Despite the amazing blessings we received during her NICU stay, we wanted our girl home and family to feel complete. Unfortunately, before that could be our reality we had another mountain to climb.

After Christmas, Amelia's little body began to tell us she was ready to have her heart fixed. Our days had moved so slowly, but suddenly we had a plan for transport back to the level 4 NICU. The next day transport came to switch her machines, a snowstorm was headed towards us that they wanted to beat. After so many agonizing weeks of waiting, we were headed up the mountain in a blink of an eye. This time the drive wasn't excruciating, because the nurse assigned to transport Amelia was family and she updated me along the way. Amelia slept her whole journey, and we traveled in a state of calm anticipation.

Fear:

We were at the second hospital for a week as the team prepared. Simultaneously seeking and dreading a procedure on your tiny child's heart is nearly impossible to describe. We had plans to get through the procedure aspect of the day, but no amount of preparation eases the constant rush of all the feelings. I was up before dawn to hold my sweet girl the day of her procedure. I struggled to let even my husband hold her before they took her back. We both cuddled her, serenaded by the playlist we made her and took just in case pictures. Our surgeon came and prayed with us, then they took her back to the operating room. My husband and I were alone in her now empty room.

The next hours passed quickly despite the anxiety generated by knowing our tiny baby was on bypass. I had prepared distraction activities that sat untouched as I couldn't focus on anything. The doctor came to the waiting room to update us, the surgery was a success, the three holes were closed. A tumultuous week followed, but she was healing and improving.

Complete:
We went home the day after my son's second birthday. My mama heart was so full and we were so incredibly happy. I had a month leave to spend with our family at home. We filled this time making memories and taking thousands of photos of our family together. Our family was finally able to meet our sassy heart warrior.

Overwhelmed:
This is where I wish I could say our journey got easier at this point but not quite yet. We were learning how to parent two kids at the same time, while juggling work, doctors appointments, therapies and so many readmissions. I noticed our son was acting out, very reserved in social situations and had strange sensory behavior. Some of his providers voiced similar concerns and we weren't sure if this was caused by the trauma of

the previous 6 months or if there was another cause. We participated in a study and he was officially diagnosed with Autism. His diagnosis story is nowhere near as long as Amelia's and in contrast it felt like being thrown straight into the deep end. Things are less concrete with autism than Down syndrome. While some things we needed were the same for both kids we were now adapting to two very differing needs. There was no time to process yet another life altering diagnosis. We moved from overwhelmed to drowning, now there were more therapies, more things to research and more demands. I love both my kids fiercely but felt guilt that I didn't make normal babies.

Expectant:

We added to the huge life changes and downsized our house and I went part time at work to accommodate doctors' appointments and therapies. After a few months, it finally felt like we were shifting out of survival mode. We definitely do not have it all together, but we are figuring it out together as we go. After nearly 2 years of processing every emotion imaginable, I am relieved to say that for the most part our days are filled with the happy joyful ones again. I am hopeful for both my kid's futures and delighted in their achievements.

No matter what challenges you face in your extra lucky journey, I know you can do it.

You are strong, you are capable and you are loved,
Colleen

Meet Colleen

Colleen is an extra lucky mama to two amazing kids. Mothering Remy and Amelia has taught her so much on advocacy, autism and Down syndrome. She is also a hospital pharmacist, avid reader and animal lover. She'd love to support anyone feeling alone on their journey and can be found on IG @ colleen.patton224.

LETTER 16
Extra Lucky Jamie

Dear Mama,

Congratulations on your baby! While my story is still very much being written, my goal is to share with you what I have been through and what I have learned so far in hopes that you will not feel alone in your journey.

I had my first child, Violet, in April of 2021; she was born healthy, with no complications. As it is with your first, you worry about everything a little more during the pregnancy. I distinctly remember at the time of the 12-week test telling my husband that no matter what we were to find out, if it was safe for me and the baby, I planned to move forward with the pregnancy, "even Down syndrome," I said. Violet joined the world at 7 lbs. 1 oz. I knew I wanted her to have a sibling (a brother, preferably) and that I was creeping up in age (38 at the time), so we decided to try for another child.

It was February 23, 2022, when I got the call; I still have the voicemail. I was at a staff retreat and stepped away to check the voicemail thinking my doctor would just say I should plan for gestational diabetes again. Never in my mind did I think I was going to receive the news that I had a 97.27% positive predictive value of having a child with Down syndrome. How? I did not even worry about the tests this time because I had a perfect little girl at home. I took the news, swallowed it, and went about my day – for me, this was not something I wanted to tell my husband over the phone and in hindsight was my best method for processing it. When I got home, my husband had an exciting new job offer and here I was about to crush his news. We went from sixty to zero in one moment. We both cried and then I was able to tell him some more news, it was going to be a boy. We felt excited and overwhelmed. We felt helpless and lost.

The next day, I contacted the MFM my OB recommended; the nurse was less than helpful, making me feel like I had a very short window to come in for the CVS (I had no clue what that was) or I would need to wait until week 16 for an amino (again, what's that?) to "help me make a decision." Slow down lady, what decision? I just wanted to talk to the doctor, and I wanted the test to be wrong.

Five long days later and we finally got in to see

the doctor. Suddenly, there he was on the ultrasound screen, our son. My husband grabbed my hand and said, "we're doing this." We knew at that moment he was ours and going nowhere. We made it very clear to the doctor that an amnio would not be necessary, and frankly too risky, our minds were made up. So started the waiting game of hitting each milestone to see what they could find "wrong" with our son. Week 20, anatomy scan: no major findings, except for an echogenic bowel and some brain cysts, which both later disappeared. Week 22, heart scan: we received a 'congrats' from the cardiologist, who cited the 50% chance of a heart defect in these patients; our son showed no signs of a heart defect. We were in the clear for any major physical abnormalities and were just monitoring the normal growth stages at a heightened level. With nothing new to report, I will be honest, in the back of my mind, I held onto that 2.73% chance that he was not going to have Down syndrome despite what every doctor and parent suggested, but I always knew the outcome in my heart.

We kept our news within our close-knit group of friends and family. We wanted people to be prepared to accept our son, but also did not want a lot of questions about things we simply could not answer. We found email and telling people face to face most effective. But be careful, some people may react differently than you think. You will learn a lot about the people you surround yourself with during this process.

John Wagner was born August 14, 2022, at 7 lbs. 7 oz. He was not too big, nor too small - he was perfect. One look into his eyes and we confirmed his diagnosis. He was also granted a second thumb (known as polydactyly and unrelated to Down syndrome). He stayed in the hospital one extra night because he failed his oxygen test twice (for those who don't know what this is, you put the baby in the car seat, and they measure their oxygen levels for 90 minutes. If they fall below a certain number, they will not be cleared to go home yet). So, in the end, we were in the hospital longer for our daughter than our son.

I am writing this as John is 8 weeks old and sleeping in his crib, swaddled and happy. We were lucky, and I know not everyone else is this lucky. I know there are NICU stays, surgeries, feeding tubes, and even losses. We also felt lucky to have found out so early, we had plenty of time to read and prepare. But in the end, prepare for what? We had no idea what our son would be like when he was born; would he have an obstruction? Would he have thyroid issues? A sandal gap toe?

Hearing and vision issues? Truth is, and this is the best advice I can give you: He is not a textbook. Your child is not a textbook. The facts and figures you are reading are a collection of generalizations from years of cases and many of the issues listed can happen to any child.

So now here I am in the early stages of a newborn with Down syndrome. Remember that your child has Down syndrome, not the other way around. What does that look like? It is a job in itself to schedule all the initial appointments (geneticist, specialists, therapists, the surgeon for his hand, and regular checkups). I want to rely on our county's offerings but know the true success stories also include additional therapy sessions, so I am learning about what our insurance will cover. I am connecting with other people in the community to learn the acronyms, best doctors, and techniques for coping with it all. Oh yea, and I am dealing with an 18-month-old who is having all the feelings about being that age as well as learning to be a big sister.

We are by no means in the clear and there is so much to come. I often fear that while we got lucky with some of the early challenges that individuals with Down syndrome face, I worry that there will be more challenges that lie ahead. I worry about how people will treat him; I worry about him "passing" every test;

I worry about his height and weight and where he fits on the scale; I worry about his life when we are gone. It is no less than I worry for my daughter, it is simply different. But then I look forward; I look forward to fewer doctor's visits; I look forward to him reaching milestones that our whole family has worked together for him to accomplish; I look forward to him telling me he loves his life and that we played a role in that. I think back to that nurse (we later left that MFM practice) and her pushing me to make a decision when the decision was made for us: we have a son with Down syndrome. We were always going to have a son with Down syndrome.

Every child with Down syndrome is different, none of them are textbooks, you will worry, but you must look forward.

You got this.

Jamie

Meet Jamie

Jamie is the proud mother of two children, Violet Marie (21 months) and John Wagner (5 months), and lives in Rockville, MD. Jamie has spent the last 12 years in the education and meetings arm of the medical association world, often balancing motherhood, work travel, and everything in between. She embraces her prenatal Down syndrome diagnosis as a gift she and her husband John were meant to receive; John Wagner has proven that to be true day-in and day-out. She hopes to promote awareness about the advances in Down syndrome care and highlight John Wagner's uniqueness in a way that gives him strength, confidence, and hope towards a more inclusive world. Jamie is available to talk openly about her experiences so far and learn about what's to come for her little guy and can be reached at jlynnparreco@gmail.com.

LETTER 17

Extra Lucky Brooke

Dear Mama,

Let me just start by saying a child with Down syndrome is the greatest gift. Your child will teach you patience, love, and pure joy you didn't know existed. Let me rewind to tell you my journey and how I can say all that with confidence to you.

It was August of 2020 and my husband Mark, and I were ready to have another child. We had our sweet Graham who was 1 ½ at the time and we thought it was a good time to try for our second. We had fertility issues, so Graham was conceived through IVF and for the second we were going to go through the process again. We made it through and got a positive pregnancy test, but when it was time for the 6 weeks scan my womb was empty and it was a miscarriage. It was very difficult, and I needed some time to regroup before we tried again. IVF is so hard physically and emotionally I just didn't know if I could go through it again.

Mark and I went on a date night in December and had an honest conversation about having another child. We agreed that we would be ok if Graham was our only child and maybe consider adoption down the road. Well unbeknownst to us, I was already pregnant by the good ole fashion way. A month later I took a pregnancy test and then made my appointment to see my OBGYN. By the time I saw my doctor I was already far enough along to take the NIPT blood test. It took two weeks to get our results, because we had the biggest ice storm to hit Fort Worth, TX in a long time. My doctor called me on a weekday evening and asked if I was able to talk. Immediately when I heard the doctor's voice, I knew something was up, because normally the nurse calls. The doctor let me know that our baby had a 90% chance of having Down syndrome and the baby was a girl. My initial reaction was of surprise from Down syndrome and excitement because we were having a girl. Mark wasn't home from work yet, so I called him and told him the news. It was all very matter of fact because I think we were both in a little shock. And I will be honest, our thoughts went to a fearful, sad place. Thinking about Graham and how it would affect him, not having a typical sibling to grow up with, what kind of health issues she might have and what her quality of life would be. We know now that these are all normal thoughts, but they are fearful thoughts that are not true. We were so thankful we had the prenatal diagnosis for us to mentally prepare. This kind of news can make you question if it will affect your marriage in a negative way. We have made more of an effort to lean on one another when it's hard and it has helped us realize even more, that we could get through this together and love each other stronger. We also know that God gifted us this child and would equip us to raise her. The peace we felt, by trusting in God, was overwhelming. And by March 21, 2021, we decided on the name for our baby girl, Sophie Elaine.

From the beginning of my pregnancy, I had to be seen by a Maternal-Fetal Medicine specialist to monitor Sophie and help us know any medical issues she might have. I had to be seen once a month. We knew early on that she had a Ventricular Septal Defect (VSD), an opening in the tissue between the heart's lower chambers, but the doctor was unable to determine the size of the opening at that time. Having a VSD is a serious condition, but Sophie was doing well. When I went in for my 27-week scan, everything changed. In addition to the VSD, Sophie now had Duodenal Atresia (blockage of the intestine) and I had a condition called Absent End Diastolic Flow (AEDF) where the umbilical cord has resistance and the flow to the baby can be insufficient. The AEDF required me to be hospitalized until Sophie could be delivered. I was only 27 weeks, way too early to deliver. All this information came flooding out of the doctor's mouth leaving me very confused and I lost it. Again, I immediately thought of Graham and how I wouldn't be able to be there for him, and how confusing it will all be for a 2 year old. Then I thought about Mark and how he was going to have to do it all on his own. I went into the hospital that day and was there for six weeks. That time in the hospital was emotionally difficult. It's not natural to be away from your child and husband for six weeks. They were able to come visit, but Graham hated the hospital room and never wanted to stay. I just kept my faith and held the fact that it was what was best for Sophie. They hooked me up to monitors four times a day to check her heart rate and make sure she was thriving. At 33 weeks it was decided that she was tired in the womb and needed to be delivered. I knew the day was coming but I was still nervous. It was all real now and we were going to have a better idea of Sophie's condition. I had a c-section because we knew she was going to be small.

She came out at 3.5 pounds screaming her little head off. She didn't require oxygen at birth, just a little tube to drain her stomach from the intestine blockage. They brought her to me all bundled up while I'm lying on the table, and she immediately calmed down and just stared into my eyes. She was so beautiful, and I knew that at that moment my life had changed for the better. The peace God had given me got me to that moment and I felt it fill the room.

She would have to be taken to another hospital after delivery to prepare for surgery for the duodenal atresia. Her surgery was successful, and she stayed in the NICU for six weeks, gaining weight and strength to go home. There were times when I was so nervous if I wasn't going to be able to feed her, because that was our biggest hurdle. I learned so much being in the NICU from the wonderful nurses who took time to teach me feeding techniques and gave me confidence. I will be forever grateful for that time and being able to hold her for hours and build that special bond. We finally got to bring her home and it was a huge weight lifted off my shoulders. Sophie thrived at home. Having our family together again was the greatest feeling and we all settled in. Sophie was the perfect addition to our family. Graham took to her so fast and loved snuggling up to her. He has loved her from day one. And I knew that because God had given Sophie to us, He had prepared Graham in ways we will never understand. Graham is a better person because of his little sister, and I know he will always watch out for her. Mark and Sophie have the sweetest bond and they love each other deeply. Everyday when Mark gets home from work, he scoops her up and spends that quality one on one time. He sings to her, and she just coos and giggles with him. It is so special to watch.

Sophie is now 15 months old and her VSD is functionally closed. We have a few more doctors appointments than I did with Graham but other than that our life is simple, and Sophie is healthy. She goes to daycare with her brother and is in a class of typical peers. She works every week with an Occupational Therapist where she works ten times harder than a typical child. She fusses when it gets hard and smiles when we cheer her on. She requires more time to meet her milestones, but that just makes us celebrate even more. She has slowed us down in a positive way and shown us what really matters. You can look at her and know she is going to change lives and make those around her better. She has already changed me and strengthened my faith. I will cherish this journey knowing Sophie is meant to be in this world to show the people around her what true love is all about.

Children with Down syndrome will do all the things a typical child will do in their own time. You won't miss out on watching them play sports, learning to swim, making friends, or learning to dance. All those things will happen if they want them to. Your life will be more "normal" than you think, and you will look back at the time you were fearful and smile because you will realize that wasn't how it turned out at all. You will be welcomed into a community of the most supportive and loving people. You will never have to be on this journey alone because the Down syndrome community will welcome you in with open arms and become your family. Let my journey encourage you and give you hope. It might have started as an uphill climb, but we made it to the peak and the view is beautiful.

With all my love and support,
Brooke

Meet Brooke

Brooke Worsham is a 41-year-old extra lucky mom living in Fort Worth, TX. She works full time for an oil and gas company. In the little free time she has, she loves to play tennis, spend time with friends and most importantly spend time with her husband Mark. She has been married to her husband Mark for nine years. They have two children Graham (4) and Sophie (18 mos.). Brooke and Mark were both born and raised in Fort Worth and love raising their family there. They are supported by both of their families and lifelong friends that live in the area. They have connected with several families with children with Down syndrome in their area and are part of a supportive community. Brooke is involved with the Down Syndrome Partnership of North Texas, helping raise money and awareness for the Down syndrome community. Her Instagram is @ brookie8103 and she would love to connect.

Extra Lucky Jennifer D

Dear Mama,

First, I want to tell you that it will be okay.

Hearing that your child is on the autism spectrum is life changing. I know—my beautiful Kya Alexandra was diagnosed at two and a half years old. This diagnosis paralyzed me with fear. Truth be told, I thought her life was over, but that couldn't have been further from the truth.

Mama, I know how you feel. That horribly dark daunting feeling is sitting deep in your soul. Your stomach is sinking at the thought of this life change. You will learn over time, as I have done, there will be a different way of parenting your child than the one you imagined. It is hard to accept but you will get there. And remember that sweet baby is still the same child you had prior to hearing this life altering diagnosis.

My daughter didn't change after hearing she was on the autism spectrum, but I did. I fundamentally changed as a person; I was angry. That's the ugly truth.

All the whys flooded through my mind: why my daughter, why me? However, I learned over time my daughter is exactly who she is and I love her with every fiber of my being, and dare I say more than I could have ever imagined?

Watching the world carry on without us was shattering. For far too many years, that is what I focused on every day in every hour and minute. That anger almost broke me, and I was resentful for so many reasons. Our Saturdays were spent in therapy instead of playdates at the park to the point where watching my friend's daughters do all the things I thought we would be doing was simply too much for me.

The phone rang less and less...it soon stopped ringing all together.

I am not telling you this to scare you. I am telling you this because I understand. I understand the deep pain and I understand every changing emotion that comes along with this life altering diagnosis. You are not alone.

I was suddenly tasked with learning about all the different therapies instead of planning birthday parties. It's as if I had to become an expert in speech, occupational therapy and so many others along the way. I was lost and heartbroken. It felt isolating and unfortunately, I learned how autism had become a money-making machine and I learned who and what mattered for programs. As we blazed through therapy after therapy and various therapists, I began to settle into autism. I had to allow myself to accept that this was forever. And through all the various therapies, two changed our lives.

Kya didn't speak her first word until she was five. She didn't chew or swallow her first solid food until she was eight. Her speech language pathologist and occupational therapist truly cared about Kya and seeing her succeed. Without their guidance, I am not sure where we would be today—certainly not here. My daughter had the potential; she just needed people to believe in her.

Can I tell you a secret? The most important piece of advice I was given was that I needed to work as hard as my daughter, if not harder. Her success sat on my shoulders and it was up to me to push my daughter and to nurture her. We became an unbreakable team. I can truly say we have bonded in a way most people will never understand.

Your carefree days will be replaced with therapy, holiday visions will change overnight and every relationship will forever be altered. For me, that was the hardest thing to accept. When the dust settles, you will have the people around you that are ready to support you and your child through this journey. And while I am handing out words of wisdom, take the help that comes your way. You will need it. I didn't take any help for years and finally accepting it was a pivotal moment for me.

Acceptance didn't come easy. I had our entire life mapped out from the moment I found out I was having a girl—a mini me. School friends, sleepovers, mani/pedis, college, marriage and grandbabies. Coming to accept that some of those may not happen was one of the hardest things I have ever had to do in my life. My head knew the reality, but my heart took many years to catch up. I struggled.

I often talk about grieving the child I thought I would have and not seeing the beautiful one right in front of me. To be honest, my daughter is twelve and I just figured this out two years ago. I sat in that grief and allowed it to chip away at me for eight long and challenging years. I soon found myself detached from the life I knew and the life I thought we would have; I didn't recognize the women looking back from the mirror anymore.

Another pivotal piece of advice I can give you is to

allow yourself time to grieve. Let yourself go through all those feelings. When I began writing about our autism journey, I often called this journey the three Ds—denial, devastation, and determination. It took me a long time to get to the last D; determination was hard. When I realized and accepted that this was our life, I knew I had two choices; I could continue burying my head in the sand or move forward and give my daughter the life she deserves.

Don't feel pressured to put your child in every therapy possible, a little bit of time here and there to process the new diagnosis will not change a single thing despite what many people—people that have never walked this journey—will tell you. I also want to tell you to be careful who you choose to work with your child. I suggest you learn about their education and how they will benefit your child, also remember they work for you...but more importantly they work for your child. In the beginning of this journey, I was desperate to help my daughter. I didn't listen to anyone and I didn't take time to absorb what was happening. In the long run that didn't do justice to her.

I also want you to know that relationships will change. If you're in a marriage it will be tested to the brink. Your family and friends will come and go, but in the end when all the dust settles your focus will be your beautiful child and moving forward. Hang in there, mama, I know your heart is shattered. Allow yourself that time, you will get there. I promise you will get there.

Of all the things I didn't think my daughter would be able to do, she does so many! One of our favorite things to do together is to get manicures and pedicures and then go for lunch. I truly never thought those things would be possible. There were many times I had to carry her through a parking lot kicking screaming and crying. Keep trying and never give up.

There is beauty in this special needs' life, it is right in front of you. When you are deep in grief remember your sweet baby is so much more than a diagnosis. Autism is forever, but so is the love you have for your child.

On We Go.

Jennifer Dunn

Meet Jennifer D

Jennifer Dunn is a single mother to her twelve-year-old, autistic daughter, Kya. They reside in Vancouver, British Columbia, Canada. Outside of her corporate job as a General Manager, Jennifer writes about and advocates for her daughter on her blog, Keeping up with Kya. She also co-hosts and co-produces the Table for Five, No Reservations Podcast. You can follow her on Facebook as Keeping up with Kya (20K+) IG keepingupwith_kya and contact her at keepingupwithkya@gmail.com.

LETTER 19
Extra Lucky Jill

Dear Mama,

I don't think either one of us, or anyone for that matter, expects to hear the words "diagnosis" or "disability" when pregnant, but here we are living those words daily. And let's be real, it is sucky some days. While the diagnosis you and I are living with may be different, I hope you know you are not alone in this journey.

My journey started in 2014 when I gave birth to my first child, a healthy baby girl we named Jiselle. We were so blessed to have an easy birth and healthy baby as we dealt with a complication at 32 weeks called Intrauterine Growth Restriction (IUGR). We brought Jiselle home on time and she was strong even lifting her head up the day after we brought her home. It was such a beautiful and loving time in our life.

Everything progressed as it should have until Jiselle reached the age of six months. We started noticing her development starting to slow especially when compared to her peers, but I think with your first baby, you are not sure what to expect and think he/she will catch up in their own time. However, as we approached ten months, the pediatrician became a tad bit concerned. Jiselle was not sitting in a stable manner, was not coming to sit, was not trying to crawl, did not want to bear weight on her legs and had a very weak core. So, we started physical therapy thinking she had a developmental delay and she will be back to her developmental age in no time.

As time passed, things did improve, but not at the expected pace. Jiselle still did not come to sit or crawl and was also not saying anything verbally, but she was getting stronger. So, we started more therapy including OT and Speech all with the hope that she will get there one day. We continued on this path for a little while longer until we were asked to see a geneticist. There was a lot that we had to deal with in that entire journey including an MRI and fighting for our right to change doctors, but finally in 2018 with a genetic blood test we received the diagnosis of Rett Syndrome. Jiselle was almost 4.

Now, don't be fooled with the calmness of the above description because there were so many tears (and I mean *so* many) throughout those almost 4 years. Questions of *why me* and w*here did I go wrong*, because

I thought I did everything right. Questions of *why is my kid not doing all the things her peers are* and *what else can I do about it* all while making sure no one is labeling Jiselle or putting her into a box. I was continuing to hold on to the hope that one day she will be able to do everything – a hope that I still hold on to. No one has told me that she can't do those things, even though I have learned that the way she does these things may look a little different. It was 3.5 years of grieving the loss of experiencing raising a child the way I expected to when I found out I was pregnant.

At some point prior to receiving Jiselle's diagnosis, I made the decision to pull myself out of my grief and choose the path of joy, because at the end of the day I couldn't control any of what I was experiencing and honestly I was so tired of crying and being sad. I was literally doing everything I could to give Jiselle every opportunity to thrive and get stronger. I had to make the decision to accept the journey I was on and move forward with my life fighting for Jiselle and for my family's happiness. So, when I received the diagnosis of Rett Syndrome my response was *ok, let's keep going* because it didn't change what we were doing or how. It only gave us more information on what to expect for Jiselle's future. Because I had already gone through the grieving process, I was able to accept her diagnosis and move forward.

Rett Syndrome is a rare postnatal neurological disorder, and while it is genetic it is rarely inherited. Rett Syndrome affects mostly girls and is caused by a MECP2 gene mutation on the X chromosome. What typically happens is a regression of skills between 6 and 18 months, including a loss of hand use and verbal words and sometimes gross motor function. I explain Rett Syndrome as a spectrum because some girls can walk and some have better use of their hands and some can say a few words so symptoms can be mild to severe. The diagnosis can come with seizures, breathing issues, and sleeping issues.

There were a lot of unknowns with Jiselle's diagnosis as this only affects 1 in about 10,000 births, but through organizations like Girl Power 2 Cure, International Rett Syndrome Foundation, Rett Syndrome Research Trust and other families, I was able to lean on resources when I was ready. I had to do this all on my own time and share this diagnosis with the world when I was ready and was able to process the overwhelming amount of information. I didn't want my child to be labeled or restricted from being able to reach her full potential so I decided I would share when I was ready.

Jiselle is still unable to walk unassisted, come to sit, use her hands, or talk, but she is a happy girl and we have been lucky to not see daily seizures or concerning breathing issues thus far. However, that does not mean that we have it easy. We have dealt with a scary hospital stay. Every time she gets sick, we have to watch her like a hawk as she cannot process mucus as a typically developing child can. So while we don't see the severity of some symptoms, we do struggle with others.

I always try to look for a positive with things in life, because I feel like things could always be worse even when I feel like I have it bad. I know that seems cliché but to me it is all about perspective. So, even though Rett Syndrome seemed like a rough diagnosis to us, a positive about it is that Jiselle and others with Retts are fully cognitive. So, the issue isn't with what is being said to her or what she sees because she can take all of that in, but in turn it is an issue with getting the answers or her thoughts or her movements out. It is like she is trapped in a body that doesn't work the way she wants it to. This means that she is able to learn and keep up with her peers, including learning to read and write and do math, but how she answers may be different than her peers. She might use an eye gaze to say yes/no, an eye gaze laptop to do homework or an eye gaze communication device to talk. I am thankful she has the ability to do all of this and so thankful for a team at school who is on board, as well as organizations like Rett University that work with families, like Jiselle and I, in learning how to communicate.

As I write this in 2022, Jiselle is 8 and in second grade. We have a lifetime ahead of us filled with questions due to her diagnosis. *How are we going to do this* or *what does this mean for Jiselle's future or even our future*, but I try super hard to not get caught up in it, especially for this Type A personality. While I never asked for a child with disabilities, it has given us many blessings and completely changed our perspective on life. We as parents are more accepting and kinder; things that mattered 10 years ago don't matter to us anymore. We take life day by day most days, and we think about how we can continue to move forward and do the things we wanted to for our family with this diagnosis, like travel. We don't have it all figured out and life is still challenging, as Rett Syndrome does bring on lots of health concerns - Jiselle might be down for the count with a simple cold - but we cross those bridges when they come.

My mom always tells me that life isn't for sissies, and you know, she is so right! We all face our challenges in this journey of life and regardless of what that challenge is. We somehow (just like Jiselle) persevere and come out stronger on the other side even when it seems impossible. My journey with Jiselle is a struggle most days, but I try to remember the joy she has brought to us all. I thank her for changing my perspective and the perspective of others she touches, because at the end of the day, life really is short and there is too much good in life to miss out on.

Love,
Jill

Meet Jill

*Jill and her husband Bailey live outside of Nash-
ville, TN with their three kids. Together they
started The Jiselle Lauren Foundation to raise
funds to help kiddos with disabilities experience
joy in everyday moments and have unique experiences by providing financial assistance to families
and organizations. You can learn more about The
Jiselle Lauren Foundation at www.thejisellelau-
renfoundation.org or find them on Instagram and
Facebook at @thejisellelaurenfoundation. Jill also
keeps a family account on Instagram that you can
follow @pratt_partyof5 to see more.*

Extra Lucky Jen Z

Dear Mama,

I am sharing my story with you to bring peace to your heart and ease your mind. I have been in your shoes and can assure you that everything is going to be ok. First, let me share a bit about myself. I am the kind of person who likes to be prepared. I have worked in corporate communications for more than 15 years and pride myself on preparing clients for events, milestones, media interviews, etc. Even on a personal level, I like to stay prepared as a way to minimize and manage stress. However, nothing could have prepared me for when I got the call from my doctor telling me our unborn child had Down syndrome.

I was pregnant with our third child and so far, the pregnancy had been going great – just like it had with our other two children, Josie and Bobby. I felt good and was working full time and managing my life and family well. On this particular day, everything was routine; I dropped the kids off at daycare earlier that morning and I was sitting at my desk having just wrapped up a client meeting when I received a call from my doctor. I thought it was strange to hear his voice, since usually a nurse or assistant would call. And to be honest, I had completely forgotten about the prenatal blood work I had done about a week prior. He quickly delivered the news that my blood test indicated a 99.9% positive result that my baby had Down syndrome. My heart sank down to my toes and I quickly walked into the hall. I couldn't comprehend what he was saying. My mind was racing as I asked him how sure he was. He confirmed that the test was 99.9% accurate. "How often are these tests wrong?" I asked. "Not often," was the reply. He reassured me that children with Down syndrome live very full lives, and the conversation was a blur from there as I tried to process.

I immediately left the office and called my husband, Bobby. I delivered the news and asked him to meet me at home. My husband was extremely supportive as we both sat on the sofa, and I cried an ugly cry. My fear came from the unknown and thoughts of what his or her life would look like and how other people would treat them. And then after about an hour, I decided I wanted to go do something "normal," so we went to

Target and strolled the aisles as we mentally collected ourselves.

That weekend, we went to visit friends in Boston. We had the plans set already and didn't want to back out. It ended up being exactly what we needed to take our minds off everything as we focused on our family and were surrounded by another loving family. The whole drive there and back, I prayed that the results were wrong. We went for another appointment; a consultation to talk to the doctor about the results. At that appointment, we brought our two younger kids along. Our doctor was extremely supportive and positive, which I am very grateful for now, after learning that this is not always the case for some. It was at that appointment when we learned we were having a girl. I was so excited and cried at the news. The moment the doctor told us the gender, it felt more real and that everything was going to be ok. I opted for an amniocentesis to confirm the results. I wanted it so that I could start fully processing the news and not think we were the one percent of people whose diagnosis was wrong. The test confirmed our baby girl had Trisomy 21. That was that. In a way, it gave me peace of mind and a path forward. Grace came over me and I felt a stronger trust in God that he was taking me and my family to a place that was going to bring us more joy than we could have ever imagined.

The next months of my pregnancy were long and still filled with stress and worry. We sold our house and bought a new one. We were already in the process of selling/buying before the diagnosis and I took it as a sign that God was putting us in a new home that was going to be even better for our new family of five. Work was busier than ever and there were not enough hours in the day to keep up with it all. The busyness kept my mind from googling and worrying too much, but as night came, the worries were heavy. Will she make it full term? Will I miscarry? What will her life be like? Will she go to a normal school? Will she date? Will this strain my marriage? Something that helped was searching for families on Instagram who were living these amazing lives with their child who had Down syndrome. I quickly discovered this supportive and positive community called "the lucky few" and I wanted in! Beyond social media, I would also advise you to surround yourself with people who are going to support you – make plans for lunches, playdates, double dates, girls weekends with people who will lift you up and do not be afraid to put distance between you and those who don't.

The weeks went by, we moved into our new home and I felt a calm come over me and my family as we settled in. The holidays quickly approached and just like that, our baby girl arrived on December 26th, two-and-a-half weeks early. Caroline Grace weighed 7lbs 11oz and when she screamed her first scream, my heart burst. She was finally here! Caroline spent three weeks in the Neonatal Intensive Care Unit at Monmouth Medical Center in New Jersey, with some of the best nurses I've ever met. While there, she received oxygen treatment until her lungs strengthened and she could breathe independently. We also realize we are very lucky Caroline did not have heart complications. On that day, and every day since, our fear was replaced with pure joy.

Caroline will be celebrating her third birthday this year. She spends her days at a wonderful daycare, where she has many friends. She receives physical, occupational and speech therapy regularly and attends ballet class at a dance studio on the weekends. She is smart, curious, kind, feisty and beautiful. We also just welcomed our fourth child, Alexandria, and Caroline has been owning her new role as enthusiastic and protective big sister! We are far from the days when we first learned of her diagnosis; I can't explain it to you other than to say, the diagnosis no longer consumed us, our minds, or our daily conversations. Sure, we deal with therapies, evaluations, more frequent doctor visits and nebulizer treatments for colds and seasonal viruses, but the heavy weight has lifted. We are living an extremely full life, as is Caroline, and we have made it our mission to educate and advocate for inclusion.

If you are navigating a Down syndrome diagnosis with a heavy heart, I hope you know that I am thinking about you. I also hope you know that the weight gets lifted. Perhaps not right away, and that is ok, but give it time for the fog to clear and for you to see how lucky you are to be on this journey. In addition to surrounding yourself with supportive people, I urge you to take a closer look at your life (e.g., job, daycare, doctors, etc.) and make adjustments where needed to create a life that works for you and your new little one. Something that helped me tremendously was finding a new job that allowed me to work from home and remain close to the daycare.

Lastly, I leave you with this...I hope you see the pieces start to fall into place. I hope people show up for you in ways you would have never thought. I hope you show up for yourself. I hope you advocate for what you need and what your baby needs. And most of all,

I hope you know that I am rooting for you and your little one! We all are.

Love,
Jen Zoller

Meet Jen Z

Jen is the mother of four beautiful children, one with Down syndrome. She grew up in St. Louis and now resides in New Jersey with her husband, Bobby and their big family. When she isn't working full-time as a mom, she works full-time as a public relations specialist in the healthcare industry. Juggling life and work is not easy, but it is so worth it. At the end of the day, it's important to remind ourselves to be our own advocates as much as we are for our children. Feel free to contact her at jenjzoller@gmail.com or on Instagram @gramercygirl.

Extra Lucky Tabitha

Dear Mama,

When I held my children for the first time, I like to describe it as a box of love opening in a place I did not know existed. I was overcome with emotion, looking at their little faces with newborn baby skin and sleepy eyes. I snuggled them in and imagined what our life together would look like. As mothers, when our children come into our lives, we are gifted with a sense of purpose, drive, and inspiration that lives in each moment we share with our children.

I had my children a little later in life, in my late 30s, as I was building a career as an attorney and spending my time working to build that career. I wanted to find balance, a word I find a bit comical at this point in my life, in work and home life. I wanted to be one of those moms who makes homemade cakes on birthdays, shuffles kids to after-school activities, and puts on a suit to fight the good fight in the courtroom.

I knew that no matter what or who my children

became, I would support and honor their spirits with my whole being. I wanted to give them a mother standing behind them during easy and hard times. A mother who would reach out a hand when the world's weight got too much to bear. I had imagined a lot of things about what kind of mother I would be and wanted to give space to figure out who my children were at their core.

Our son, Nixon, was our first baby. He came into the world swiftly at 33 weeks and four days by emergency c-section. Our parenting journey started with professionals surrounding us with advice, timelines, and suggestions on how we could support our son through those first couple of months of life. I immediately felt like I had failed him - feelings that still surface from time to time. I know that the failure of my body, the inability to carry him and protect him for the hoped-for 40 weeks, was not something I had control over, yet somehow I felt like I had failed from the start. Our birth experience was shared between the two of us and what seemed like 10,000 medical professionals. These outside parties involved in our parenting are something that has carried through as a common thread through all the years of our children's lives.

As we found our way away from the hospital with

cords, beeps, and late-night suggestions from nurses, we started to find our rhythm with each other. I started to gain confidence as a mother, and we began to melt into a routine. I continued to work and juggle the hats I wore as a professional and a mother. I often felt that the balance was impossible; I did not know how other women seemed to make all the parts of their life work so easily.

As time passed, we started discussing with daycare providers and school programs about Nixon's development. I began to struggle more and more with the elusive balance. He had a speech delay. We sought early intervention and began having more people come into our home to teach us how to support him. After numerous discussions, we got on the waitlist with a developmental pediatrician to obtain a developmental evaluation, and I began to hit the internet to search for answers. We did not have anyone directly say that what they were seeing could be autism, but it was hidden behind the words of numerous appointments with providers.

I again felt those feelings of inadequacy. That somehow, I, just who I was, was not set up to live in all the parts of my life that needed an extreme amount of focus and attention. That I couldn't find the sweet spot of balance that I saw around me from so many other mothers. What I began to learn as I talked to other mothers was this was a feeling most of us have. In the sleepless nights, wondering if we are doing things right for our kids. In the push and pull from the outside world and the walls of our homes.

During this time, I would often watch our son Nixon and take him in. The beautiful boy he is, with his sweet spirit, full of smiles, and happy demeanor. I wondered if he was too young to carry a diagnosis for the rest of his life.

As we waited for Nixon's appointment with a developmental pediatrician, I became pregnant with our second child, Nora. Since our daughter was conceived, the experiences with Nixon put me in a place of wondering and watching. The pregnancy with Nora was wrapped up in fear. Would she make it to full term? Would we end up with an emergency like her brother and have a NICU stay? I also wondered how I would find the energy, focus, and strength to parent two children. Would she gain language and skills in line with the checklists every new parent receives? Would we have more appointments and providers in our life?

On January 16th, 2020, after several appointments with the developmental pediatrician and a psychologist, we received Nixon's formal autism spectrum disorder diagnosis. I walked around in a fog, struggling to find my way in work, mothering, and processing what this meant for our son. What I understand now is that the wondering, the anger, my desire to protect him from the world, and a diagnosis, were wrapped up in fear and misunderstanding. I knew nothing about this part of him and wished that, at the time, I knew so much more.

As we went through this process with Nixon, Nora developed right on track, walked, talked, and gained skills right in line with those checklists. Then at around 18 months, we felt a shift. She lost all of her words completely. No sounds, no babbling, nothing. The silence was breathtaking. We enrolled her in early intervention and started seeking a formal evaluation.

On December 16, 2020, our daughter was also diagnosed with an autism spectrum disorder. I walked out of that appointment holding our daughter's hand, knowing so much more than I had 11 months earlier when our son was diagnosed, yet I still felt similar feelings as I did the day our son was diagnosed. The fear centered around how it would be possible to balance two children's needs and my life as a working mother. Fear about my ability to provide and nurture the way I thought I should be able to do as their mother. I walked away knowing with finality that this was a part of both of my children, but still not sure if I was enough for them.

Autism is now a big part of all of our lives. I don't consider it separate from my children as human beings. It is a part of who they are. Their diagnosis has changed me as a person. The feelings that I felt, and at times still feel, were necessary to help my process of letting go of my expectations about what our life was going to look like. I did not know that when my babies were placed into my arms, and that box of love was opened up, that I was just the mother they needed. That who I am as a person, and who they are as people - diagnosis included - is the beauty and gift of mothering.

I have walked away from many things in my life and said goodbye to parts of my career, and what I realize now is that it was necessary for me. It isn't easy to say goodbye while making moves to fit all parts of our life together. I often think back to my early feelings and my misunderstanding of mothering in general, and I am grateful for the view I have now.

The thing is, I have made a couple of those home-made cakes, I have taken my kids to swim lessons, and I have won cases in the courtroom after becoming a mother. Some of those parts of me have faded over time. I have also found out that I am the mother who will draft 20 e-mails to make sure services are in place, that I will take off my shoes and dance in the rain, I will carve pumpkins, watch sand fall from my kid's hands, let my kids hair run free, and celebrate with my whole heart each skill they learn. I have learned that who I am is just what they need. They are where the magic lives every day. Autism is a part of all of that, and autism is also a part of who my children are.

What I want to say is that the balance I imagined as a mother, attorney, wife, friend, and so much more wasn't where I found success. What ended up being important was growing, learning, and reshaping as I found my way into motherhood. The ability to understand my children for every inch of who they are, with the outside world looking in, is what I have succeeded at. I have learned that those feelings of failure aren't because I am inadequate as a mother. Those deep feelings live in a fantasy of expectations that I had created for myself, and the real success is understanding that what is here, the experiences we have had, are our story. It is part of our journey and has directed us to a place where what truly is important is in focus. The threads of who I am as an attorney and a mother blend into the person I need to be to support my children.

What I want to say to the mother reading this is to hold your head up high. No matter what you are feeling at this moment, that is ok. Sometimes you look at your children and are overcome with such beauty that tears will hit your cheek. You will have times when your spirit is so tired after weeks of appointments, evaluations, or feelings that you do not know how you will muster up another ounce of energy to make it through the day. When you sit across from a professional as they talk about your children or comfort in a time of distress, you will dig deep to find that energy.

What I wished someone had said to me is that motherhood is filled with complex and mixed feelings and that the deep rich love you feel for your children will carry you through the hard days. Sometimes we are shaped by our life in a way that leads us to a destination we couldn't have known existed, so there was no way to know what you would find once you get there. This is motherhood.

From one Mom to another,
You will find your way,
whatever that looks like for you.
Tabitha Cabrera

Meet Tabitha

Tabitha Cabrera, Esq., recently moved from Arizona to Montana. She spent her career as an Attorney and has recently been working on finding what is important in this life; Friends, family, and growth. She shares about her two sweet autistic children, Nixon age six and Nora age three and the family's journey through diagnosis. She has found a passion in advocacy and paired this passion with her brother Mike Barnett to publish four children's books. Available on Amazon, "Do You Talk the Way I Talk?" "Me and My AAC." "What's the Commotion with My Emotions?" and "¿Hablas Como Yo?" "Can I See Autism?" She believes that each day you have the opportunity to spread a message and extend a hand to those in need. She also shares about her perspective and journey with the ladies of Table for Five, No Reservations podcast found on any streaming service. You can find Tabitha's blog at www.peaceofautism.com,
Facebook: https://www.facebook.com/peaceofautism
Instagram: https://www.instagram.com/peaceofautism/

Letters 22-28

LETTER 22

Extra Lucky Stephanie

Dear Mama,

I too am a mother of a medically fragile child; I know this new journey you are on can seem frightening and so unknown. I know you are probably thinking that no one understands what you are going through and that you are alone. In a way you would be correct, every child's journey is so different, but know that there are people who have walked a similar road and would love to help.

When my husband and I started down this journey with our son, I felt so alone. We knew two other families, but their journeys were different from ours. Social media wasn't a big thing then, so we didn't have many groups to turn to for help. Before I explain our journey, please know that there is a tremendous amount of parents, not just mothers, but fathers who are willing to listen, help and even guide you through some of the steps you and your family are about to take.

Let me tell you a little about our story.

Payton was born October 8th, 2014. He was a week early, but no signs of anything being wrong. He had jaundice, which is fairly normal, especially compared to what we would wind up going through. We live in Oklahoma and had Payton at a hospital over an hour from home. We had to make several trips a week to get blood work done to check his Bilirubin level. We thought this was absolutely horrible at the time, looking back now I feel silly considering what we were about to endure with our son.

I noticed that when I would breastfeed, he would twitch, it started in his hands, then his arms. We were told it was "just his nervous system developing, nothing to worry about." A few short days later Payton's whole body started shaking. I remember it so vividly, watching your child have a full-blown seizure is not something you can ever forget. Payton was admitted to the local Children's hospital, where we were told everything was fine, that his MRI looked *normal, just one side of his brain was smaller but that's no different than one foot being small than the other.* We were told he would just grow out of the seizures.

Payton continued to have countless clusters of seizures daily. He had one in the neurologist's office and the doctor made the call to have Payton admitted to

Le Bonheur Children's Hospital in Memphis, TN. He explained that Payton was having infantile spasms and we needed to stop them, or they'll do irreversible damage to his brain. So, my husband and I went home, started packing and then drove over 500 miles to Memphis, TN. We had to be at the hospital to check in bright and early Monday morning. I remember sitting in the waiting room, looking around at all the other children and looking at my tiny perfect 3-month-old wondering why we were there. We were terrified, but I can remember telling my husband that we didn't need to be here, that Payton was going to be okay. We were young parents about to embark on a journey we knew absolutely nothing about.

Payton had multiple scans and tests done, and at the end of the day his epileptologist walked in and delivered news that we never thought we would ever hear, a diagnosis that no parent would ever expect. He told us that Payton had bilateral polymicrogyria, a type of brain damage where the ripples on the brain are much smaller and closer together. They told us that the images we brought from the children's hospital back home showed the same thing, even though the doctor in Oklahoma told us everything was completely normal. He then told us that it was caused by lack of oxygen to the brain and that Payton had suffered a stroke in utero. Hearing this news felt like an out of body experience, how was this even possible?! Why did this happen?! So many questions raced through our minds. As the mother I felt like it was all my fault, I kept replaying my whole pregnancy in my mind over and over, trying to figure out what I could have done that might have caused this. We were assured that nothing I did caused this, there was no explanation as to how this happened and that sometimes things like this unfortunately just happen.

We spent a week at Le Bonheur and were sent home with a medication called ACTH, which we had to inject into Payton's thighs twice a day. Everyone called it "the miracle drug" but unfortunately it didn't stop the infantile spasms and he was still having hundreds of seizures a day. We went through countless medications, a special diet called the ketogenic diet and several more hospital admissions. Nothing was stopping the spasms, so at 6 months old Payton underwent a brain surgery called a left frontal lobectomy to remove the frontal part of his brain. It was during the 3-month hospital stay that followed that we also discovered Payton was aspirating everything, including his saliva.

Right after Payton's brain surgery he caught the

adenovirus, his lungs were full of fluid and he couldn't breathe on his own, so he was placed on a ventilator for almost a month. I continued to pump but eventually had to stop, the stress of my child fighting for his life was taking a huge toll on my body. I remember feeling like a failure because I could not breastfeed my baby or pump anymore. I wish I had someone tell me what I'm about to tell you. You my friend are not a failure in any way, "fed is best" even if that means through a tube in your child's stomach or through a central line in their chest, which is how Payton gets his nutrition now.

When we were finally discharged, Payton was still requiring oxygen because his lungs were damaged, he had undergone a major brain surgery, an emergency shunt revision surgery and a G-tube placement surgery. It was terrifying leaving the hospital for the first time, not only were we first time parents, but now our tiny baby required so much extra care and we felt so unqualified. How were we supposed to take care of a child who needed such critical medical attention? We didn't have a choice but to adapt and keep moving forward. Little did we know that Payton's care level would only get more critical the older he got.

Our journey has been anything but a smooth road. Since the first hospital stay, Payton has undergone countless surgeries, hospital admissions, procedures, multiple other diagnoses, and unforgettable moments. Our journey has been emotionally, physically, mentally and financially draining, but it has also been beautiful beyond words.

Many years ago, my husband and I made a promise to each other that we were in this together no matter how hard this journey got. That we were going to be Payton's biggest advocates and give him the best life possible.

Listen to what I'm about to tell you very carefully my friend, it is okay to grieve the life you had envisioned while still feeling unbelievably blessed to care for your child. I know that with each diagnosis comes a whole new set of worries and challenges, but have faith in knowing that you are more than capable of caring for your child. It's okay to ask for help and know that you are not alone, mama.

One thing we have learned along the way is to find joy in the journey and to never give up. Trust your mama gut - it is normally spot on - and advocate for your child, you are their voice (it's okay to speak up and tell a doctor no).

We live our life one day at a time and, more often than not, one moment at a time. Remember to always celebrate the little things and never take anything for granted. Most importantly know that God created your child for a purpose, and they deserve so much love. I will always be in your corner; you got this mama!

Stephanie

Meet Stephanie

Stephanie Stanley is a wife to an amazing man and a mama to a warrior. She stays home with their son while her husband travels for their family business. She and her husband are both Payton's full-time caregivers.
Instagram & Tik Tok - steph_stanley12
Facebook - Prayers4Payton

LETTER 23
Extra Lucky Jennifer M

Dear Mama,

Riley's story starts April 23, 2019. We had opted to get the 3-month scan and NIPT test with our 3rd pregnancy just for the extra ultrasound. The tech brought in the Maternal Fetal Medicine Doctor and he pointed out that there was an increased nuchal translucency measurement and that it was common with different trisomies, he suggested we have the materNit21 test to see which specific trisomy we were at high risk' for. We opted for it.

I got the call a few days later that the baby was at high 'risk' for trisomy 21, otherwise known as Down syndrome. I'm not going to lie, it took my breath away. I cried for what I thought I was losing and I cried because of the way the news was delivered from the genetic counselor. She delivered the news as if it was a terribly awful condition. Then of course I had to go back to Maternal Fetal Medicine where the specialist suggested I get an amniocentesis or a CVS (Chorionic villus sampling), in case I would like to know 100%, if I had plans to terminate. That was obviously not an option for us. We said we will have this baby no matter what, it hurt me that they would even suggest something. I just couldn't fathom their reasoning... why? I have a teenage nephew with Down syndrome. What if my sister-in-law aborted him? HOW was he not worthy of life? HOW is my baby not worthy of life?

The rest of my pregnancy was very stressful, to say the least. I had terrible morning sickness, high blood pressure and a high risk pregnancy. I had 2 fetal echo-cardiograms which were inconclusive.

Fast forward to October 10, 2019 (my 35th Birthday) when I had another ultrasound. The OB told me I had an umbilical vein varix and that I had to be induced ASAP because I was at risk for stillbirth.

On October 11, 2019 at 12:15 am, Miss Riley came into this world! She was just perfect. She cried right away but then her color started to become gray, so they took her to the NICU and gave her oxygen. We had a week stay in the NICU and also a diagnosis of an AVSD heart defect that would need surgery. They told me also that Riley had a few characteristics of Trisomy 21. I told them I was aware there was a high chance of that early in my pregnancy and that it didn't matter, she was the most perfect baby in the world.

In February 2020, Riley's heart got the repair it needed. It was a bumpy road and we ended up with a second surgery to place a pacemaker, but since then we started to really see the real Riley. She is a force to be reckoned with. I truly believe the world will know her name.

Down syndrome, heart disease and being born a month early has NOT held Riley back, she is meeting her milestones and wants to be a big kid like her big brother and big sister! It is truly amazing to see how strong Riley is. Despite her low muscle tone, she is rocking PT, doing baby signs and getting into everything like any toddler should! I do know we will have some challenges ahead, but I also know that Riley is a rockstar and she will overcome them all!

Riley will be starting preschool in a general education setting all while receiving the therapies she will need. Riley being fully included is not only great for her, but it also is for the other children. Riley will teach them so much!

Down syndrome isn't something to be feared, it is something to be celebrated! Riley has opened up a whole new world for our family. Riley's smile can warm even the coldest heart, her determination is nothing short of extraordinary and her extra chromosome makes her who she is! She IS Riley and she HAS Down syndrome.

You got this!
Jennifer

Meet Jennifer M

Jennifer McCormick is a stay at home mother of 4 from the North Shore of Boston, Massachusetts. She enjoys spreading love, acceptance, and inclusion of people with Down syndrome on her social media. Down syndrome and other disabilities are nothing to be feared, she wouldn't change her daughter for anything in the world. Find her on her Instagram @jmccormick526 or email her at mccormick52612@gmail.com

LETTER 24

Extra Lucky Lisa

Dear Mama,

"I don't want her. I don't want her. I. Do. Not. Want. Her." is what I said to my OBGYN at my 6 week follow up appointment after my daughter was born. A child we wanted and tried for and were overjoyed to be pregnant with.

On the day Lauren was born, while I was in the recovery room from my c-section all hopped up on morphine, a doctor came in and started saying, "We think something chromosomal might be going on. She's small and has thick eyebrows and long eyelashes and a full head of hair…" I stopped listening after that but the long list of things "wrong" with her continued to be rattled off by the doctor. I was thinking, "How could those things be bad? She sounds beautiful!" and the doctor continued, "We have to take her to the NICU. She must have tests done." I was in disbelief and shock.

The next day I heard the words Cornelia de Lange

Syndrome (CdLS) for the first time. While my baby was in the NICU on another floor in the hospital I started doing the one thing none of us should do, but that we all do anyway, which is look it up on the internet. There is very little information online about CdLS and what is available is very dated and very bleak. I searched images of CdLS, and I thought all these babies and children were so ugly! How could their parents stand to look at them much less love them! Horrible right?! What was wrong with me on a fundamentally human level that that is what I was thinking?!

I was discharged after 4 nights in the hospital and had to leave Lauren behind in the NICU. Leaving the hospital without her was so surreal. Once home, a deep depression took hold. I did not go visit Lauren for a week while she was in the NICU. I couldn't leave my bed. I wasn't eating or drinking, yet I was getting sick around the clock. I considered being admitted to the psyche ward but when I found out it would have been in a different hospital than where Lauren was, I didn't want to make things harder for my husband.

And the thoughts. All the thoughts. I was completely consumed with thinking about CdLS and Lauren and our future. How am I going to mother her? How could I meet her medical needs? What is having her going to do with all the plans we had for our future as a family of four, the way we wanted to live our life? Could we be a part of our community and society and go places or out to eat or even travel? How would we have to accommodate her needs? How challenging would it be to go…anywhere? Would she be able to go to school? Would we have to move? I basically wrote off doing anything other than going to doctors appointments and convinced myself I would be house bound with her. I felt like I was given a lifetime prison sentence.

I'm not a crier, but had gotten quite excellent at it in the midst of all this. What I cried the most over is how this would affect her older brother. He also now has a lifetime of having to live with this disability in his home and have it be a part of his life. How would having her impact him? What if his friends didn't want to come over because of his weird sister? My heart broke for him not just once but over and over as I imagined terrible scenarios of how having a special needs sister would affect him.

I've talked to moms who, when upon hearing their child is something other than "healthy and typical", responded with resolve or their faith to right away say, "This is the baby we were given and we're going to love them and care for them and do right by them." I've always been incredibly jealous of those that handled it like that because I immediately went off a steep cliff. All I saw was darkness and despair. I didn't choose to have a special needs child, but I have to care for her. I didn't sign up or volunteer for this but I'm fully responsible for her well-being. It's not what I wanted and now I'm getting a crash course in all things medical; different specialties, tests, medicines, procedures and surgeries.

Lauren came home after a month in the NICU and my confidence was shot. I didn't think I could be her mother. I didn't think I could meet her needs. I was scared of her! Between my husband being off and family, someone was here 24/7 the first month she was home, but eventually they all had to go back to their other lives and responsibilities. I was still afraid of her and didn't want to be alone with her! Along came my dad who truly saved my life and sanity by coming over every day 8 hours a day for months to feed, change, and be with Lauren while I found my way out of my depression, and until my confidence grew enough that I wasn't scared to be alone with her. I am eternally grateful for the kindness, compassion, and love he gave to us.

In time, and with the help of medication, therapy, and loving family and friends, I slowly realized we just needed her to be a baby at that moment. We just needed her to eat, sleep, and poop! And if/when she'd meet milestones and what our future looked like wasn't as important as Lauren being as pain free as possible and content/happy day to day. Anything else beyond those two things was gravy!

I had quite a revelation at some point along my journey. I had always been mothering her well despite how terrified I was. Three out of the four weeks she was in the NICU I did spend hours with her a day. I rocked her, I sang to her, I made sure she was comfortable. All things that just instinctually happened. Once she was home, I was on top of her feedings and recording every ounce she ate and made sure to total it for the day for the doctors to review. I made and kept doctors appointments and we showed up to every one and did whatever next thing that particular specialist wanted us to do. I sang to her and made sure she was comfortable and offered her toys and stimulation and interacted with her like I had done with my son.

With time and healing I could finally see how beautiful Lauren was. I could finally see what she was capable of instead of the things she couldn't do. My number one goal for Lauren was to make her the best version of her we could, whatever that looked like. No comparing her to other children her age or even other children with her syndrome. I finally realized she was the perfect daughter for me and I'm the perfect mother for her and am so happy she was born to me. I want her! I want her! I want her! 1000 times over I want her, and I want to be her mommy and for her to be my daughter!

So, mama, you got this. No matter how scared you feel, how much you do not want this to be your life, how much you wish this was a dream (nightmare?) you could wake up from, there is light and love and joy and unbridled happiness waiting for you.

All my love,
Lisa

Meet Lisa

Lisa Wrigley Lewin is a happily married mother of two who lives in southern New Jersey. In 2013 she gave birth to her daughter Lauren who was diagnosed with Cornelia de Lange Syndrome (CdLS) at birth based on physical features of the syndrome. Gene testing a few months later confirmed that diagnosis as Lauren had a gene mutation on the NIPBL gene which happened spontaneously at conception. As time went on and Lisa's new role as a mom to a disabled child became more normal, Lisa's interest in making connections with people propelled her to become very active on the CdLS discussion board online and with the CdLS Foundation (www.cdlsusa.org) connecting with families newly diagnosed and sharing her daughter and their journey with them. Lisa hopes by sharing her truth and journey, in all its raw honesty, that if she can make just one person not feel so alone in their feelings, she'll have put out some kindness into the world.

LETTER 25
Extra Lucky Lora

Dear Mama,

Twenty years ago, when my grandmother was under hospice care, I overheard my aunt describe the journey of caring for her through her final days with these words, "This is my greatest life's work. I was created for this." As I have walked through the journey of parenting children with disabilities, beginning with my foster care and adoption journey that started 16 years ago, I have repeated these words to myself. I share them with you, so that they can become part of your mantra as well…"This is my greatest life's work. I was created exactly for this."

I was 24 years old, single, a relatively new pediatric occupational therapist, living in a new city, just having started a new job at a children's hospital. It started how most love stories start…I met a girl. She was the sweetest and sassiest four-month-old girl, with no teeth and no hair. She loved Elmo and long walks in the hospital hallway. She just so happened to have a type of very aggressive cancer called infantile leuke-mia, and an unstable birth family situation. This family situation continued to unravel during her time in the hospital, until it became clear that she was going to need to leave the hospital with a foster family. Her situation was unique – with so many medical challenges and a high likelihood of life-threatening or life-limiting conditions, she needed a foster family who could take on a child who may not live, but if she did, would certainly face a lifetime of medical and developmental challenges. She needed a foster family who wanted her, exactly her, exactly as she was.

I remember the moment that I realized that person was me, just as I'm sure you can remember the exact moment that your life changed, as you realized (through whatever path you came to parenting) that you were now going to be a parent of a child with a disability. I remember hearing my aunt's voice in my head at that moment, "This will be my greatest life's work. I was made for this. I have exactly what it takes, and I want exactly this child. I was made to be this child's mama." Many people doubted my decision, because I was young and had limited life experience, and at times throughout the process, I doubted myself too. But ultimately, I knew that this was indeed my calling in life, and that I was made for this journey. That does not mean that this journey was without challenges. Over the next 3+ years as we journeyed from foster care to adoption, and over the past 16 years of raising this baby/child/young lady, I found out things about me I had never known.

I *thought* I was already strong. That was until I watched this little girl suffer chemotherapy treatments and surgeries and come out swinging and ready to take on the world. I thought I was already strong until I sat outside a courtroom during a termination of parental rights hearing, not sure what to ultimately hope and pray for, because both paths came with their own set of worries for this little girl I loved so much. I thought I was already strong until I was brought to my knees by the chance to be her forever mom, just days before National Adoption Day in 2010.

I *thought* I was in charge. That was until I had to ask permission from the state to go visit my own mother, because doing so while I was a foster parent meant leaving the state and flying with a child who, though I was raising her, was not legally mine. The same went for cutting her hair, changing her school arrangement, or taking her to a new doctor, until the day that I was able to legally adopt her. I thought I was in charge until the first time that feisty three-year-old turned and looked me in the eyes and said, "No. I don't WANT to sit down. I WON'T sit down," and I realized I was truly powerless to make her do a single thing she didn't want to do in life.

I *thought* I was "alone" on this journey…until the first time she got septic and my mom jumped on the first plane to sit with me by her bedside, because a foster grandchild is the same thing as a grandchild, and of course "Lovie" had to come to the rescue. I thought I was alone until a three week hospital stay, when I had no paid leave left at work after her many complications, so other moms from work, church, the oncology floor, my local "disability moms support group", and all other walks of my life came out of the woodwork to take 4 hour shifts to sit with her in the hospital so that I could work. I thought I was "alone" until I looked around me outside the courtroom during the termination hearings and there were 15 friends, family members, and medical professionals that had treated her for years who were present there to support me, to support *us*. I thought I was alone until I looked around me inside the courtroom during adoption day and counted 25 people we knew personally who were there just to support us in our transition to being a brand new legal family.

I *thought* I knew love...until the first time she laid her head on *my* shoulder after a medical procedure, because I was her ultimate comforter now....until the first time her tiny hand slipped into mine of her own volition when it was time to cross the street, because I was her protector. I thought I knew love until the first time I heard her new legal name spoken aloud in the courtroom, with finality.

As I sat down in front of my computer to write this letter, trying to figure out what to say to you, Mama, about my journey and to inspire you on your own journey, I looked back at a private blog that I had written during the years of foster care and adoption, to keep our family and friends updated on her medical battle and legal proceedings. I poured my heart out paragraph after paragraph, opening my heart for the people who cared about us. I have always been an angsty and emotional writer, but never as much as in the days before the final termination hearing and the adoption that came just three weeks later. You see, Mama, over the years while I thought I knew everything, and learned that I knew nothing, I did learn everything about the most important thing...the little girl who was entrusted to my care. During those years, I became not a parenting expert, but an expert in my daughter. In the twenty days before the final termination hearing, I wrote a small series on the block called "T-minus."

"T-minus 20 days until court: Did you know…M has 4 birthmarks on her feet? When she was a baby, I thought one was a splinter and tried to take it out for ½ hour. Did you also know that if I have to put M's oxygen on when she's already fallen asleep, she shakes her head side to side? This is best stopped by sitting her up before I try to put it in."

"T-minus 17 days until court: Did you know…that M rubs one eyebrow when she's nervous or tired, and two eyebrows when she's really sick, uncomfortable, or scared?"

"T-minus 7 days until court: Did you know that M has an unbelievable knack for languages? She picks up and remembers sign language words, Spanish words, and many English words far beyond her age level? Not bad for someone who started out non-verbal! Did you also know that she can pick her nose with her tongue?"

As I looked back on those words and the anxiety behind them, I realized that at that time, I was so desperate to share all that I had learned, all that I knew about this little girl. I wanted to share the things that nobody else knew in case the termination did not go in my favor, and I never got the chance to share those things about her again. Three weeks later, the blog looked completely different: calm, serene, full of hope. In a letter to my daughter on the blog a week later, I described my gratefulness for the chance to parent her forever: "You are such a blessing to me, and to anyone who enters your life. You are articulate, albeit perseverative. You are cuddly, in your own sensory-defensive way, and you save the best ones for me. You have a deeper understanding of the world around you than any preschooler I know. And you are my daughter; just ask anyone who has seen us together. You have my mannerisms, my intonation, some of my facial expressions. [Your adoption day] was an amazing day, by far the best day of my life. At some point, you may have to share that distinction with future siblings, but for the time being...best day of my LIFE. I promise to do my absolute best to make everyone (especially you) proud of the mom I am, the mom I want to be for you. I love you, and you are mine."

So, Mama, I want to repeat those ever-important words that I said at the beginning of this letter, with one important addition... "THIS is my greatest life's love, AND my greatest life's work. I was made for this," and the same goes for you, Mama. You have already done so much work, to arrive at this day, sitting here with this book. You have already had moments of heartache, pain, joy, bliss, and love. You have done the best of times and the worst of times. There is still hard work left to come, because parenting is HARD. I have a teenager now (among other children), so I think I'm qualified as an expert in hard! Despite the hard, I hope you go forth and live your greatest life's LOVE. You were made for this.

Lora

Meet Lora

Lora is a mother of three girls, one of whom was born with a rare form of childhood cancer, and another who was born with a developmental disability. Her first daughter came to her through the beautiful/brutiful process of foster care adoption. Lora is a pediatric occupational therapist and is now a manager of a busy rehabilitation practice at a large hospital center. She is a state-trained advocate for people with disabilities in the state of Virginia. In her free time, she enjoys singing and writing, and hopes to one day write a book about her experience with adopting a child with a disability through foster care. Her most important job is raising her daughters to be strong self-advocates and is raising all of her children with the understanding that everyone belongs, and everyone deserves a seat at the table. She currently resides in Northern Virginia with her 16-year-old daughter, Marz, her 5-year-old daughter Riley, her 2-year-old daughter Abby, and her husband and mother.

LETTER 26

Extra Lucky Johanne

Dear Mama,

Congratulations on your baby! Your baby will be able to learn and do so many things and will do typical kid things. I'm a woman in her late thirties who has Down syndrome. As a child I was involved with school clubs, girl scouts, dance, played soccer, basketball and softball. In middle school and high school I did stage crew for the school play, played field hockey, tried track and field, was a part of making the homecoming float, was in the parade, helped with teaching Sunday school and did choir and piano lessons. Also starting in high school and for many years after high school I worked in a library which I loved. School was hard, but I always persevered and did well. The social aspect of school was also hard for me; I had my small group of friends but when it came to gym class, recess and extracurricular activities I would be picked last for things, be not included in things and I wouldn't be invited to most parties and events from my peers like the other children would be and I would get bullied. All this and the bullying always made me feel small and like I wasn't good the way I am and I used to feel it was my fault when I would experience bullying, but I have come to learn through the years that when people don't treat me right it has nothing to do with me and everything to do with them. I feel I'm a strong person with everything I've been through this far in my life; when your child experiences this just be there for them and let them know how special they are just the way they are. Always tell them to never change for anyone, I will never change for anyone. If someone can't treat me right or accept me for who I am, then I am done with that person; I never used to be that way but things I've been through have taught me this and it's a way to show our own self- respect and a way to start learning to love ourselves the way we are. No one should feel like they need to be different from who they are to fit in; you've got this.

After High School I went on to community college and got my associates degree. I've mentored for the Dream Program at Mercer County Community College in New Jersey and have loved it. My dream in a job sense has always been to be a teacher; even though that isn't my reality I feel I'm pretty close to it with my mentoring and through my podcast called Inclusive Views. You can check Inclusive Views out on Instagram, Facebook & Tiktok; the podcast can be found on my website at www.inclusiveviewspodcast.com, Spotify or on itunes. I graduated from NJ Partners in Policymaking in 2021 and can't wait to see where I can go with this for all people with disabilities; so far since graduating I have helped with a safety grant, and am a part of the Ambassador program for the National Down Syndrome Society. The idea of my podcast started when I was going through NJ Partners in Policymaking because I want to share my policy and advocacy journey and show people that people with disabilities can and do contribute to our communities and deserve to be treated with dignity.

My mom is my best friend and I couldn't ask for a better mom. I have the best little sisters and love being an older sister and I have an awesome brother-in-law and love being his sister- in- law. I'm an aunt to an amazing niece and that's my favorite part about my life. I just want to be the best role model and aunt for my niece. I am also a dog mom. My niece and my dog keep me going. I feel so grateful, and I can't imagine my life without my dog and family. I feel very lucky to have had the best Poppy and Grandma. They always made me feel like I was good the way I am and were always there for me and just like my mom, they were always my biggest supporters.

I enjoy helping my dog's dog rescue with their social media accounts, with getting volunteers for adoption events and with volunteering with different things. Besides the rescue, I love writing, watching my favorite T.V. shows (a favorite is The Voice), watching movies, going to concerts and conventions, talking and hanging out with friends, drawing, painting, crafting, reading, doing yoga, riding my bike, going on walks with my dog and many other things. I love joining a lot of things and being active and that will never change.

I feel proud of all my accomplishments this far in my life and how I don't let my challenges stop me from trying different things. Everything I go through and all my challenges shows me what I am made of and I'm proud of the fact that I don't let anything knock me down for good and I never will let that happen.

What I want people to realize is that people with Down syndrome are people first, we have the same hopes and desires like everyone else. Having Down syndrome doesn't mean it's the end of your child's life and that one shouldn't expect anything from them; yes, things will have to be altered with expectations put on them; challenges and roadblocks throughout their life will always be there, but it doesn't mean that they can't lead productive lives. Having Down syndrome isn't all of a person, it's only a part of them, and shouldn't be seen as the only thing of a person. It should also be embraced.

Your baby will amaze you and will be such a blessing to your family. Don't treat your baby differently from other children you may have; we don't like to be treated like that. We are just like any other child and no child should feel limited and should be free to try what they like. Never be ashamed of your baby. Just know the best thing you can do is to love your baby.

Sincerely,
Johanne

Meet Johanne

Johanne Mayer is a self-advocate with Down syndrome and an Ambassador for the National Down Syndrome Society. Johanne graduated from the NJ Partners in Policymaking and works to try to change legislature and policies for individuals with disabilities. She founded the podcast, Inclusive Views Podcast, to shine a light on discrimination and help create a more inclusive world. In spare time, Johanne dedicates time to animal rescue in honor of her fur baby Nellie (learn more about Nellie on Instagram @nelliejazzed). You can find Johanne on instagram @inclusiveviewspodcast or on her website inclusiveviewspodcast.com.

Extra Lucky Monica

Dear Mama,

In March 2022, we welcomed our 3rd child, Isaac, to our growing family. We had waited to find out our baby's gender until birth, since we were already blessed with our oldest daughter, Lily, and our youngest (at the time) son Louie. We had an emergency c-section due to the risk of uterus rupture at 37 weeks.

After the rushed operation, we saw him being pulled out and my husband announced joyfully to the OR - "It's a BOY!!" We were absolutely overjoyed. He was here! Healthy and crying loudly for all to hear. They carried him over to me after they had toweled him off for me to do skin to skin with him. I was in complete awe of this new precious baby snuggled on my chest.

While in recovery, they brought us our baby. He's swaddled up tight and I asked my husband to show me the pictures he had taken in the OR. As I'm scanning through the pictures I noticed one particular picture where the nurse had held him up - they had just put ointment on his eyes. The shininess of the ointment made his eyes just pop. Something about his eyes just looked different, thin and more almond shaped. I took note in my head but didn't think anything else of it.

I started to try and get him to nurse. I just kept praising God for taking care of us through the surgery. My husband asks to look at our son's ears, and then his hands. I can tell he was looking at a list and I could see the wheels turning in his head. I asked him what he was looking for - it was obvious he was looking for something. He said very calmly, "I think he has Down syndrome." The moment he said it, I knew he was right. His eyes in that picture made so much more sense now. We were now going down the Google list for Down syndrome markers together. He had every one – almond eyes, palmers' crease on both hands, neck fold, flat nose bridge, and tiny folded ears.

I can honestly say, I was at peace. My husband and I are firm believers that all life is God-breathed. God created our baby perfectly, just as he was. We would love him and were there to protect him – just as our other babies we had been blessed with! Now that we knew he was a boy, we started talking names. We had a short list but we weren't firm on any of them.

Isaac – "he will laugh," "reflecting the laughter."

We love the story from the Bible about Abraham and Sarah. Sarah laughed in disbelief when God told them that they would have a child. It was a perfect name.

That was it. That is what his name was going to be, and he was ours. This was just the beginning. That evening, and for those 3 days of recovery in the hospital, we deep dove into all there was to learn about Down syndrome.

The next few days in the hospital would be filled with so many conversations between pediatricians, nurses, social workers, occupational therapists, and lactation consultants. These were conversations that were very different from when we had our 2 typical children. We knew then we needed to know all that we could about our new diagnosis so that we could ensure Isaac received the best care and resources.

Flash forward: Isaac is now 9 months old. Here are a few things I've learned since his birth.

A diagnosis does not equal value. Society, family, or cultural preconceived opinions may try and say otherwise. When we first shared Isaac's diagnosis, the comments and unsolicited advice were painful. Reflecting back, I'm confident these comments were not ill intended, but they were uneducated. If anything, a diagnosis is just a characteristic. A characteristic that is part of our being in how God made us, and it is not anything to be shameful of, but rather a special characteristic of what makes us innately unique.

Being present is a gift. Isaac has always moved at his own pace. His milestones look different. However, because his pace is different, it has forced us to tap our breaks and soak in the present moments. It took him 4 months before he smiled and for those first few months, we eagerly waited to see his sweet smile. When he finally smiled, that wait was worth it!! These moments make us appreciate and celebrate every small joy and win.

There is beauty in resiliency. When we first realized Isaac had Down syndrome, we knew he would need more individualized attention. I worried about how his diagnosis would impact our other children. Would they be jealous? Would they be gentle enough? To our surprise, our two older children have been obsessed with him since the day we brought him home. You can usually find our rambunctious son jumping all over the place, but with Isaac he is soft and always holding his hand. Our daughter, she's like a mini mama and my biggest helper – singing to him, getting his paci, and telling him stories. They see all the therapy sessions and doctors appointments he attends. They may only be 5 and 3 but they cheer for him every time he lifts his head up during tummy time or grabs a toy. They see him pushing through the hard to achieve the goals set in front of him. By the sound of their cheers, you would think Isaac just won an Olympic gold medal. They are seeing the beauty in resiliency. They are watching, real time, that some things in life, you have to work towards, and it won't happen overnight. They see that if you keep working hard and you don't give up, you will make your goal.

You know your child better than any doctor or specialist. When Isaac was 8 months old we noticed his oxygen was declining quickly while he was sleeping. We rushed him to the ER to be evaluated. They evaluated him, gave him a breathing treatment, a chest x-ray and they decided to discharge him. I knew in my mama heart that he was still struggling to breathe. His oxygen had continued to dip anytime he descended into a deep sleep. I refused to be discharged. The on-call pediatrician was not happy about it. I had 2 nurses, a doctor, and a social worker try and convince me to just leave and come back later in the night if his stats didn't improve. But I couldn't ignore my baby's signs so I stayed. After his oxygen dipped 3 times in an hour we were finally admitted and that one night stay turned into an 8 night hospital stay with an upper respiratory infection. Don't let others doubt your motherly instinct. God has given us parents these instincts – use them.

Community can be a safe haven. Our community has been so encouraging. Strangers have prayed for us when we were in the hospital. We have received doctor referrals and medication recommendations when needed. We have had several care packages sent with books, information, therapy toys, and blankets when we came home from the hospital. You are not alone. God didn't intend us to live this life alone, he created church and community for life's journey.

Isaac has changed our lives for the better. We see life through a whole new perspective. A perspective of gratitude, resiliency, and love. I'll forever be grateful God trusted us with Isaac. He knows we are capable. He knew we could handle it; we couldn't handle it alone. But we will be able to handle it with the Lord guiding us.

Monica Mangiacapra

Meet Monica

Prior to becoming a stay at home mom in 2019, Monica worked as a Program and Operations Manager where she oversaw the South East Region of the United States for one of the largest healthcare companies in America. She and her husband, Louis, have been married for over 12 years, and together for over 18. They call Texas home and they have 3 children: Lily, Louie, and Isaac. They enjoy road trips together as a family and volunteering with their local Down syndrome Nonprofit, The Upside.

Extra Lucky Taryn

Dear Mama,

I do not know where you are on your journey, but I thank you for being here. My daughter Rhea was born with Down syndrome and a congenital heart defect in 2020. Her heart condition, a complete AV canal defect, was successfully repaired through open heart surgery when she was just two months old. My story won't be the same as yours, but I hope that it can give you whatever you may need right now.

I was a mom to three little girls when I found out I was expecting my fourth daughter. This little girl was one surprise after another, and, up until that point, I was someone who did not like surprises. Not one bit.

I had worked really hard on my mental health for years after becoming a mom. It took me a long time to learn ways to deal with my need for control and my habit of projecting. I would project the worst case scenario in any situation (the desire to control would then come into play) and let myself become a ball of anxiety. I let myself believe lies I told myself about how something would be. I was living in the future way more than anyone should.

Through therapy, exercise, yoga and meditation, I dug myself out of that. I learned how to live in the present and I learned what my mind and body needed to be the best version of me.

Then, five little words threatened to undo it all.

"Your baby has Down syndrome."

Those five words put me back in the future. I started letting myself believe the lies I was telling myself about how this would go. It took until my daughter, Rhea, was born for me to gain some perspective and snap myself back into the present.

I want to share these lies with you here. The lies I told myself, that you may be telling yourself now too. The lies I let myself believe until I remembered that living in the present is so much more beautiful than living in the future.

This child will be a burden to her siblings.

This was the number one lie I told myself. I let

myself believe that choosing to have this child with Down syndrome meant that I was also choosing a harder life for the three daughters I already had - both now and in the future. It took me about 30 seconds into seeing my girls meet for the first time for that belief to vanish. The reality is that the bond between them is not dependent on them being the same. I know that their love runs deep enough to withstand hard times, and I believe in my heart that Rhea will always bring so much more into their life than she will take. My older girls have learned a different level of compassion and already think of things in different ways – ways I may not have been able to teach them otherwise.

Everything will be harder for our family.

Is life busier now? Have there been hard or stressful times? Yes, and yes. But do I think of our family life as hard? No. Parenthood can be hard. Life can be hard. Rhea has not made it that way. If anything, she has helped me tune in to a deeper way of living. She has shown me what's important. She has taught me that what I used to stress about doesn't matter. She brings so much joy into our lives that I almost can't believe I ever thought she would make it hard.

I won't be able to manage everything.

Parenting a child with a disability does come with a lot extra. Extra appointments, extra therapy, extra worry. When you look at this in the beginning, it feels like a mountain to climb - an impossible one. I looked at my busy life and thought "how can I possibly add to this?" But, before I knew it, it just became part of routine life, so much that I don't even think about it much. However, I learned, and I hope you will learn, how to have boundaries for when it becomes too much. It is ok to say no. It is ok to take a "therapy break" (in fact, some of my favorite therapists support it!). It is ok to know the days where another appointment would push you or your child over the edge, and call it off. Start over the next day, it's okay mama.

We will never get to be "empty-nesters."

A big part of parenthood is preparing your children to "leave the nest" someday. When you have a child with a disability, it can feel like all of those dreams for the future are blurry, or maybe the dreams completely disappear.

The truth is, there's no way to tell what the future

will look like. However, one day after Rhea's diagnosis, while I was down a mental rabbit hole about the future, I thought about my grandparents. My beloved grandparents had a daughter who suffered from alcoholism. She never really left home and her disease put them through *hell*. When she was good, she was great, but when she was bad, she was *bad*. She refused to get help, despite their efforts. They were good, loving parents and yet their daughter had a disease none of them could conquer.

This example may be extreme, but thinking of them reminded me that there are no guarantees when it comes to our children's future. My neurotypical children would not be spared from the trials of life just because they have 46 chromosomes versus their sister who has 47. They are not guaranteed to go to college, get great jobs, get married, get pregnant and live an easy life. We have decided what a successful future looks like, and not everyone fits into that mold *and that's okay.*

Worrying about the future seemed fruitless, unless I was going to worry about *all* of my children (which of course, we all do anyway!). And beyond that, thanks to the hard work of parents who came before me, so much is changing for our children with disabilities.

There is so much more opportunity for our children to live fulfilling lives, and I don't think we can predict - or project - what that looks like.

My life will never be the same again.

This one, my friends, wound up being true. However, the way I was saying it then and the way I say it now is very different. In the depths of my grief I believed that everything ahead of me would be hard. I believed that I would become a shell of myself, and lose so much of the things I needed to thrive.

Yes, things can be hard. I'm not dismissing the day-to-day things that are harder for Rhea, and for myself. *But hard is not the same as bad*, and my gosh, I would not change a thing. The people I have met, the experiences I have had, none of it would be possible without Rhea. None of it would be possible without leaning into the hard days. Above all, the greatest joy is walking through life with my family, including this little girl who fits perfectly into it. We would not be us without her and all that she teaches us.

So mama, write down your "lies" and then also write why they probably aren't true. Let life surprise you rather than decide how it is going to be. You may not feel prepared, but you are fully equipped.

You've got this.

With love,
Taryn Lagonigro

Meet Taryn

Taryn is a wife and mom to four daughters, the youngest of whom threw her into a world of advocacy when she was born with Down syndrome in March 2020. Taryn is the owner of Four Clovers Publishing and the author of Ups, Downs and Silver Linings. Taryn is the co-owner of Iris Yoga, a yoga studio in New Jersey, and Extra Lucky Moms. Taryn is certified in yoga and meditation and also volunteers for several Down syndrome organizations and non-profits, including the Down Syndrome Diagnosis Network. Taryn's writings have been featured in several national publications and she has frequently been a guest on podcasts and television shows for topics relating to yoga, Down syndrome and parenting a child with a disability.

Acknowledgements

Thank you, first and foremost, to Brianna, Jessica F, Sarah J, Cara, Elena, Jaime, Amanda, Kelly, Michelle, Sarah R, Erica, Ashley, Elizabeth, Colleen, Jamie, Brooke, Jennifer D, Jill, Jen Z, Tabitha, Stephanie, Jennifer M, Lisa, Lora, Johanne and Monica. This book would not exist without your vulnerability. Your willingness to tell your story will help moms for years to come and will help change the landscape of diagnosis and support. You are all amazing advocates for your children, and we are proud to stand shoulder to shoulder with you in this community.

Thank you to Morgan, Mary, the Booknook team, Carley Storm Branding - thank you for your contributions in bringing this book to life. We are grateful to get to work with people who believe in our mission so much.

To the Extra Lucky community, which started as an idea that YOU turned into a community. Thank you for all you have taught us about your amazing children. You are who keeps us motivated to keep our mission moving forward.

To Addie and Rhea, thank you for inspiring every

single step of our journey. It is an honor of a lifetime to not just get to be your mothers, but to get to watch your friendship blossom.

From Jess:

To my heart and soul; My family: Matt, Charlee, Adeline, Mom, Papa, Britta, Christian and Dad. Thank you for the incredible support you have all shown me, always. Not many get the family I was blessed with. I will never know how to thank my stars for your love. Thank you for loving Adeline the way I needed you to.

To Mom, Britta and Christian: The family that got me through it all. The family that loves and supports all that each other holds dear. The four of us are my heart. I love you.

To Matt: Thank you. Thank you for loving me the way you always have. Thank you for pushing me to my unlocked potential. You are the partner dreams are made of. I love you.

From Taryn:

Raff, thank you for always believing in me, I feel your pride daily, and I love you.

Sofia, Layla, Genevieve and Rhea, thank you for reminding me every day why I do what I do. You are each perfect exactly the way you are.

Dad, thank you as always for being our rock. Did I tell you I loved you today?

Lauren, thank you for wanting to shout Rhea's worth just as much as me.

To our collective friends in the disability community, all of whom we probably wouldn't know if not for our children, thank you for your friendship, love and support from the moment we met. We have never known women quite like you and count our blessings every day that we get to.

To the Down Syndrome Diagnosis Network and the Stepping Stones School in NJ, we have both of your organizations to thank for our personal friendship. Thank you for cultivating environments where moms can feel supported in the early days of diagnosis.

Thank you to Jordan's Guardian Angels, Rock the 21, The Candlelighters, Alivia, A Buddy Just Like Me, The Jiselle Lauren Foundation, Ethan and the Bean, Brittany's Baskets and Gigi's Playhouse. You supported us from day one, sharing our posts, contributing content, collaborating and more. We are so inspired and motivated by the work you do and hope we can all keep doing it together for many years to come.

To Cindi (Taryn's mom) and Terry (Jess' best friend Ashlea's mom), who this book is in part dedicated to. You were advocates before it was a movement, and you never gave up on the two people who needed you most. We lost each of you right as our own advocacy journeys were beginning and can't imagine the countless things you would have continued to teach us. Yet, we know that so much of you is already in us; you were an example before we ever knew we would need it. It's because of women like you that change has been made in this community, and we will take it from here, in your honor.

About Extra Lucky Moms

Jessica Quarello and Taryn Lagonigro, who both welcomed children with Down syndrome in 2020, found immediate support and connection from the Down syndrome community after welcoming their daughters, but kept encountering mothers of children with other disabilities who were missing that same level of community.

Tapping into their backgrounds in non-profit, marketing, and business, Quarello and Lagonigro founded Extra Lucky Moms in May 2021. The organization celebrates children with Down syndrome, autism, Jordan's Syndrome, trisomies, heart conditions, and many more through their blog, social media platforms, in-person events, apparel and accessories that give back and brand and non-profit partnerships. Their story has been shared on large media outlets such as the Today show where their brand and efforts were highlighted. Extra Lucky Moms is a place where everyone belongs, and no struggle is too big or too small.

You can connect with Extra Lucky Moms at www. extraluckymoms.com or on Instagram @extraluckymoms.

Made in the USA
Monee, IL
02 May 2023

32852145R00152